The Christian & The State

Viewed Principally Through The Prism Of
Marriage, Divorce And Remarriage

Allan Turner

ALLANITA PRESS

PUBLISHING

THE CHRISTIAN & THE STATE
© 2009 by Allan Turner

Published by Allanita Press

Cover design by Stephen Sebree, Moonlight Graphics
Printed in the United States of America

ISBN 0-9777350-4-4

For information:
Allanita Press Publication
585 Cox Road
Roswell, Georgia 30075

Most Scripture quotations are from the Holy Bible: New King James
Version, Thomas Nelson Publishers © 1964, 1965, 1966, 1971, 1975,
1983. Used by permission.

Dedication

This book is dedicated to Anita (Reich) Turner, the girl I met, went to high school with, and thought terrific some forty-eight years ago. Five years later I had the opportunity to date and get to know her. I realized quickly that I loved her and wanted to spend the rest of my life here on earth with this one great love of my life.

After overcoming her initial reluctance, she agreed to be my wife. I have loved, and been loved by, her for some forty-three years now, continuing to believe that, except for becoming a Christian, marrying her was the best decision I've ever made.

About her I can safely say that her worth is "far above rubies."[1] She has watched over her household and has never eaten the bread of idleness. Her children have all grown up to call her blessed; her husband also, and he praises her. Many daughters of Zion have done well, but in my estimation, she excels them all. Charm is deceitful and beauty is vain, but a woman who fears the Lord, she shall be praised. Consequently, she has been given the fruit of her hands, and her praise is well-known to that royal priesthood of which she is a very integral part.[2]

It is to her, my wife, my friend, the mother of my children, and the "granny" of my children's children that I dedicate this book on a subject that she and I have discussed on many occasions. Marriage, divorce, and remarriage, which serves as the prism through which the subject of this book is viewed is a topic she and I have always taken very seriously.

May her tribe increase, and may she continue to be blessed as she honors God in the things she does.

---

1 Proverbs 31:10a.
2 See Proverbs 31:27-31.

Table of Contents

Preface

Although this is a book about the Christian's obligation to the State, it will seem to some, perhaps even most, to be a book more about marriage, divorce, and remarriage. This is because the issues surrounding marriage, divorce, and remarriage can be viewed as a tool (in this case, a prism) which the author employs to explore and critically examine the subject discussed in this book, which is, when all is said and done, the Christian's obligation to the State as viewed through the lordship of Jesus Christ.

I employ the prism imagery in the subtitle of this book to help illustrate that the spectrum of views that revolve around the subject of the Christian's responsibility to the State are better understood by the several views that manifest themselves on the subject of marriage, divorce, and remarriage. For sure, there are other subjects that could be used to illustrate this point, and we will be discussing some of these. In fact, a few of these were even addressed in my first two books, *The Christian & War* and *The Christian & Idolatry*, both of which were published back in 2006.

Nevertheless, I remain convinced that the subject of marriage, divorce, and remarriage, when viewed from what God says about it and what the State actually thinks about what God has said about it, best serves to demonstrate the complexities that comprise the Christian's obligation to civil government. I believe this is true of marriage, divorce, and remarriage primarily because it is a subject fundamental to the human race, as all of us, in some form or fashion, are effected by these.

Therefore, it is best for one not to think this book as primarily a personal defense of a controversial position on marriage, divorce, and remarriage. For to do so would be a serious mistake. Instead, this book is precisely what it purports to be—an examination of the Christian's duty to the State as viewed principally through the prism of marriage, divorce, and remarriage. This means that, in the end, our understanding of the Christian's duty to the State in every facet ought to be enhanced by the arguments and examples presented in this book, and this whether you agree or not with my particular interpretation of the marriage, divorce, and remarriage passages found in the Bible.

However, and this almost goes without saying, if you do disagree with me concerning my defense of a particular position on marriage, divorce, and remarriage, which I'll be explaining in some detail during this study, you will be more inclined to disagree with me concerning the conclusions reached in this book relating to matters affecting the Christian's obligation to the State.

This book, the fourth in a series, will be the longest I've written. This is not because I have not tried to make it shorter, for I have worked diligently to do so. In fact, it has been pared down from its original 300-plus pages. Although the culled material was thought important, I eventually concluded, after some serious deliberation, it was not absolutely necessary to the material presented here. Invariably, a study of this sort will raise more questions than it answers, and the redacted material was an effort to both anticipate and answer at least some of these. These questions and answers ought to be pursued by all who are genuinely interested in this subject. Consequently, I pray you will be motivated to seek the answers to the questions raised in your mind by this study.

But no matter what your ultimate conclusions may be on the Christian's obligation to the State, or even on the subject of marriage, divorce, and remarriage, I hope you will judge this effort to be forthright and honest, for I have worked hard at making it so. As pilgrims and sojourners, whose citizenship is in heaven, our duty to the State and its inhabitants, who are, in turn, our neighbors, is difficult and fraught with dangers as well as opportunities. It is my prayer that this book will be of some help in avoiding the dangers and facilitating the opportunities.

Allan Turner
Roswell, Georgia
November 2009

Chapter 1

Starting At The Beginning:
Thinking Through The Limits Of
Delegated Authority

I n Matthew 28:18, Jesus said, "All authority has been given to Me in heaven and earth." Therefore, Jesus is not just some crown prince, as some Christians are wont to argue. Instead, He is nothing less than "Lord of lords, and King of kings."[1] The only one excepted from His authority is God, the Father, who gave it to Him in the first place.[2] Thus, as we begin this study, it is important to understand that with the exception of Jesus and His Father, the exercise of all authority is derived or delegated authority, and that this has direct bearing on the subject to be discussed in this book—namely, the Christian's obligation to the State.

But instead of proceeding directly to the State and the Christian's obligation to it, it will be helpful to view this subject in light of two other God-ordained relationships. The first of these is the Home, which the Bible makes clear was created before the State. Consequently, it is most reasonable that the exercise of authority in the Home is foundational to understanding the requirements and limits of any and all delegated authority. The second of these

---

1 Revelation 7:14.
2 1 Corinthians 15:27.

relationships is the Church. This divinely ordained institution is by no means of lesser importance than the Home and it is dealt with in this order only because it was instituted long after the Home and the State, although it is clear it had been in the mind of God even before the foundation of the world. So with this order in mind, let us now turn our attention to the Home.

The Home

By use of the term *the Home*, we're talking about the husband and wife relationship plus children, if the relationship be so blessed. It is within this first of all earthly alliances that we are originally introduced to delegated authority. But before proceeding any further, it's important to define some terms. According to Webster's *New Collegiate Dictionary*, authority is defined as the "power to influence or command thought, opinion, or behavior." For the theist, only God innately has this kind of power. In other words, because He is who He is, namely, the Sovereign Creator of the Universe, all lawful authority inherently resides in Him.

While here on this earth, Jesus made it clear that His heavenly Father had invested Him with "all authority," and that it naturally followed that the only one excepted from His authority was the Father who "put all things under Him," as we learned in 1 Corinthians 15:27. Thus, one ought to have no problem understanding that it is from God, and God alone, that all legitimate authority derives, and that all such derived authority is, by definition, "delegated authority." Consequently, the human authority we will be talking about in this study, whether it has to do with the Home, the Church, or the State, is always *limited* authority and, as such, can only be used within certain God-ordained parameters.

As previously noted, the very first articulation of this kind of authority is assigned to the Home, and this after mankind's fall into sin. In Genesis 3:16b, God said to the woman, "Your desire shall be for your husband, and he shall rule over you." Thus Eve, as a direct consequence of her sin, was told her husband would rule over her. However, and this is essential to understanding this point, her sinful condition is not the *only*, or even the *primary*, reason for her subjection. This is made clear by Paul in 1 Timothy 2:13, when he said, "Adam was formed first, then Eve." Thus, the primary reason given for a woman not to *teach* nor *exercise authority* "over a man" is the creation order itself, which is something that can only be attributable to God. So with this truth in mind, let's spend some time thinking about this created order and what it tells us.

Because the Bible says Adam was created first and existed for some time before Eve, it is reasonable to conclude that God did not create Eve to be Adam's leader. Before creating Eve, God's declaration in Genesis 2:18 seems to make this clear: "It is not good that man should be alone; I will make him a helper comparable to him." God then took Eve from the body of Adam (i.e., formed her from a rib taken from his side) and presented her to him. It was then that Adam declared her to be "bone of my bones, and flesh of my flesh."[3] Thus Adam, the "Man" (Hebrew *Ish*), called her "Woman" (Hebrew *Isha*) because she was taken "out of Man."

Consequently, Woman Was Second And Secondary, Not First Nor Primary

Using this truth as the foundation of his argument in 1 Corinthians 11:8-9, Paul says: "For the man is not from the woman; but woman from man." In other words, both her origin and name are

---

3   Genesis 2:22-24.

derived from man and are thus *second* and *secondary*, not *first* nor *primary*. When it comes to the Home, then, the husband (man) exercises his headship over his wife (woman) because God ordained it to be this way, and this was so even before sin entered into the picture. This runs absolutely contrary to some folks' thinking, for they think the wife is to be subject to her husband *only* because of sin. But as we've seen, this is simply not the case.

However, and this is extremely important, man's role in fulfilling the mandate of Genesis 1:26-28 is not fulfilled apart from the female's role. Consequently, the chronological order of creation does not just make her subject to her husband, but it also makes her a vice-regent as well. This means she is not in any way, shape, or fashion, his slave. She is to be respected as an equal, created in God's image, who, at man's side and under his loving direction, fulfills the God-given task of subduing the earth, which is certainly to be included in what was said about the husband and wife relationship in Ephesians 5:25. As things were originally planned by God, man *and* woman, as a family, a unit, a team, were to *explore* (not exploit) and *control* (not destroy) the earth. But unfortunately this plan was marred by the sins of both Adam and Eve, as Genesis 3 informs us.

Something Happened That Changed Everything

Before sin entered into the world, Adam and Eve, respecting each other's role, would have worked together in harmony to fulfill the divine mandate and would, no doubt, have eventually begun to populate the earth. By doing so, they were both operating within the authority of God. Unfortunately, acting independently of her husband, Eve surrendered to Satan's temptation and ate the forbidden fruit. This is certainly no compliment to Eve, but what happened next is no endorsement of Adam either. Eve was deceived, but not Adam. Instead, at his wife's behest, he willingly disobeyed God. As a result, both the man and woman were cursed by the Creator for their sins.

The curse on the woman is found in Genesis 3:16, and says, "I will greatly multiply your sorrow and your conception; in pain you shall bring forth children; your desire shall be for your husband, and he shall rule over you." Notice that there are two effects of this curse on the woman. First, the pain she would experience in child-birth would be greatly increased. Second, there would be tension between her and her husband. It is to this second effect that I want us to focus our attention.

When Adam and Eve sinned, their relationship was distorted. The foretelling of this can be seen in the statement, "...your desire shall be for your husband." Just what this means has been much misunderstood. Some have thought it to be referring to the woman's sexual desire for her husband. But such a desire would already have been part of her makeup as a sexual being, and this before sin ever entered the picture. Therefore, such a position does not appear tenable. The original intention of God was that Adam and Eve would bear children and fill the earth. God made the man and woman two completely different sexes; therefore, sexual desire is not perverted nor distorted, as some have suggested, and within the marriage relationship is, according to Hebrews 13:4, both "honorable" and "undefiled."

What, Then, Was Her Desire?

Well, if her desire was not sexual attraction, what was it? This, I think, can best be understood in connection with the rest of the verse, which says, "And he shall rule over you." Many, thinking the desire of the woman is co-ordinate with man's rule, believe this is describing a *harmonious* relationship that would naturally exist between a husband and his wife. Another way of saying this is that these folks believe the wife's desire is an instinctive disposition to be in subjection to her husband. I have heard this view set forth numerous times in Bible classes of which I was a part. Others, certain so-called "Christian feminists," understand this passage to be the description of how man, "degenerated by sin, would take advantage of his headship as a husband to dominate, lord it over, his wife."[4] I believe both these views to be a misunderstanding of the passage.

This misunderstanding occurs due to what I believe is a mistranslation of the Hebrew conjunction in this passage—a mistranslation that uses "and" (a coordinating idea), rather than "but" (an antithetical concept). Thus, I am convinced the correct translation should read: "And your desire shall be for your husband, *but* he shall rule over you."[5] The conjunction *but* indicates there would be friction between the husband and wife. This can be understood in connection with an identical Hebrew construction in Genesis 4:7b. Both passages use the word "desire" and a comparison of these two passages ought to give us an understanding of what the woman's desire really is.

3:16b "Your desire shall be for your husband, **and** he shall rule over you."

4:7b "And its desire is for you, **but** you should rule over it."

---

[4] Letha Scanzoni and Nancy Hardesty, *All We're Meant To Be: Biblical Feminism for Today*, 1974, page 35.

[5] For a more in-depth study of this point, see *Recovering Biblical Manhood & Womanhood*, John Piper and Wayne Grudem (editors), 1991, particularly chapters 3 and 20.

In Genesis 4:7b, sin is depicted (personified, if you will) as one who crouches at the door waiting to take hold of or capture its victim who, in this case, is Cain. Notice the parallels between this verse and Genesis 3:16b: "And unto thee shall be his [sin's] desire, and thou shalt rule over him" (KJV). Now, the NKJ version of 4:7b reads, "And its desire shall be for you, but you should rule over it." It seems clear that the idea God was conveying to Cain was that sin was a power that desired to rule over him, but he must resist and subdue it. When compared with this verse, Genesis 3:16b can be understood to be teaching that, as a result of her sin, which was a rejection of her husband's rule, as well as the rule of God, a battle of the sexes had begun. Contrary to the harmony that once existed between Eve and her husband, she would now have an inclination to exercise control over him. Therefore, if he was going to exercise control over her, as his headship demanded, it would not be without a struggle.

In other words, just as sin's desire was to have its way with Cain, God has given the woman over to a desire to have her way with her husband. Because she usurped his headship in the temptation, she is subjected to the misery of competing with her rightful head. This is, after all, justice (i.e., a measure-for-measure response to her sin). Thus, in becoming sin-sick, the willing submission of the wife and the loving headship of the husband were corrupted. The woman's inordinate desire to usurp her husband's authority would have to be mastered by her husband, if he could. Consequently, the rule of love established in paradise was replaced by a battle between the sexes that has produced an endless stream of usurpation, strife, tyranny, and ungodly domination.

Furthermore, the curse upon Adam would further exacerbate the friction that would exist between the man and his wife. The difficulty of toiling out a living would cause physical and psychological stress that would ultimately be carried over into the man's relationship with his wife. The time necessary to eke out a living from the cursed earth would force the husband to spend much more time away from home. As a result, his wife might very well feel like she was being neglected. In addition, the jealousy many husbands feel concerning their hard-earned paychecks, even though marriage is to be a joint effort, has served to intensify the battle of the sexes down through the ages. In many marriages today, the husband has *his money*, the wife has *her money*, and "never the twain shall meet." Obviously, then, the negative effects of the husband trying to make ends meet in a world that resists him on every hand are very much with us, even today.

The Curse And Its Effect

The history of man and woman, as well as our own experiences, demonstrates the real problems created by the consequences of our first parents' sins. The unity God intended for His creation was destroyed by those sins and, as a result, the woman would desire to usurp her husband's rule. At the same time, the husband, if he was to rule, would do so with some degree of difficulty. Add to these consequences our own sins, and the battle between the sexes has actually grown into a full-fledged war. The family, the very fabric of our society, is being destroyed today. Divorce is rampant. The so-called "traditional family structure" is being redefined to include unmarried couples and homosexual liaisons (they call each other "housemates," "significant others" and now even "marriage partners," thanks to the State of Massachusetts and the other states that are following in its footsteps).

In addition, the feminist goal, which is nothing short of social, political, and cultural revolution, is having a dramatic impact in our day. Whether we like to admit it or not, feminism has converted our culture to the feminist mind-set. In fact, the feminization of America is in full-swing. As a so-called "Biblical feminist" has noted: "Feminism since the early 1960s has begun to color interpersonal relations, the language we speak, family life, the educational system, child-rearing practices, politics, business, the mass media, religion, law, the judicial system, the cultural value system, and intellectual life."[6]

Paradise Lost

As originally created, the male and female were to complete each other as they enabled the other to fulfill the God-ordained purpose of procreating and subduing the earth. Neither was to seek the other's position, but as half of a whole *they were meant to complement each other*. When sin entered the picture, their distinctive roles were blurred and their harmonious relationship distorted. Instead of working together in unity, they began to compete with each other. Instead of reflecting the glory of God, they began to mirror the corruption of sin. Their original "oneness" was replaced by a power struggle that has continued in society ever since. This struggle, although it does not always manifest itself overtly, does, nevertheless, lie just below the surface in even the best of marriages.

It is most unfortunate that so many men, even Christians, "hardened through the deceitfulness of sin,"[7] have engaged in the practice of "lording it over" their wives. On the other hand, and at the same time, many women, even Christians, have become "silly women laden with sins"[8] and have not willingly submitted to the headship of their husbands. It is sad, but true, that many

---

6   Quoted in Mary Pride, *The Way Home*, 1985, page 12.
7   Hebrews 3:13.
8   2 Timothy 3:6.

Christians, both male and female, instead of "prov[ing] what is that good and acceptable and perfect will of God,"[9] are actually being guided by current secular values. Of course, Christians, of all people, ought to know that the answer to this problem is not to be found in current secular thought or even in so-called traditional thinking. Instead, the answer is found in God's word. Thus, it is in the Bible, and the Bible alone, that we will find the answers to all our problems.

Paradise Restored

A very important part of the "good news" of the gospel of Jesus Christ is that what was lost in the Garden of Eden can be restored in Christ. As faithful followers of the humble Galilean, the husband and wife can once again become the *unit* God intended them to be from the very beginning: the husband, the loving leader who "nourishes and cherishes" his wife, as if she were his own body,[10] and the wife, the suitable helper, who willingly submits to her husband's guidance "as to the Lord."[11] Obviously, such a relationship must be characterized by selflessness, yet it is *only* in Christ that one learns to crucify Self. It is *only* in Christ that one exchanges the egotistical "I am" of sinful pride for the loving guidance of the Great I Am. It is *only* in Christ that two people will live in the estate of matrimony as God truly intended.

Does this mean that people who are not Christians are really not married? No, it does not. Does it mean that a Christian cannot marry a non-Christian? Again, no, although it is certainly appropriate to argue that such a decision may not be the wisest of

---

9   Romans 12:1.
10 Ephesians 5:28-29.
11 Ephesians 5:22.

choices. Well, then, what does it mean? What it means is that with-out the restoration that comes "in Christ," marriage will never be what the Lord created it to be; *namely, a relationship of unity that supersedes every other earthly relationship and in a very wonderful way reflects the unity that exists between Christ and His Church.*[12] This Bible truth is a part of that light that illuminates a lost and dy-ing world.[13] And it is this truth that functions as some of the salt that preserves our decaying society.[14] Consequently, if Christians aren't living this truth out in their lives on a regular basis, then they're no good to themselves or anyone else.

Delegated Authority, Contrary To What Some Think, Says Nothing About Superiority

Because men and women are made in the image of God,[15] they are equal bearers of the divine image. This means that both men and women are equally human beings. Thus, women are not infe-rior members of the human race, nor are they to be viewed as somehow being second-class citizens, as they were in this country for years, and still are in many countries around the world.

Furthermore, women must not be counted as second-class citi-zens of the kingdom of God either.[16] The Bible makes it clear that they are full members of the church of Christ—i.e., the universal body of the saved; namely the "My church" of Matthew 16:18—with access to all the spiritual rights and benefits of such membership. In other words, one cannot be kept from the saving

12 See Ephesians 5:22-33.
13 See Matthew 5:14.
14 See Matthew 5:13.
15 See Genesis 1:27.
16 See Galatians 3:28.

blood of Jesus Christ by his or her *nationality* ("neither Jew nor Gentile"), *status in society* ("neither slave nor free"), or *gender* ("neither male nor female"). All human beings are absolutely equal in that they are privileged by the Grace of God to become "children" and "heirs of God" through faith in Christ Jesus.[17] Consequently, the context of Galatians 3:28, contrary to what the so-called biblical feminists among us think, deals with *who* can become a Christian, which includes everyone, and on what basis, hearing and obeying the gospel, not with male-female roles *per se*.

It is, therefore, unfortunate that so-called "Biblical feminists" have pounced on Galatians 3:28 as the touchstone that tests any interpretation of Scripture. Some have even called this passage the "Magna Carta" of all humanity. They claim it teaches it is God's desire to see all sex roles completely obliterated in the Home, State, and Society in general, which includes the Church. Equality, they falsely reason, means getting rid of all role distinctions. "Equality and subordination are contradictions!," they proclaim. They feel that "true egalitarianism [equality] must be characterized by what sociologists call role-interchangeability." They argue that any subordination is "psychologically unhealthy" and totally "carnal."

These "Biblical feminists" have bought into the feminist argument that true equality means monolithic, undifferentiated role-interchangeability, and they have done so *lock, stock and barrel*. Therefore, any Bible passage that does not square with their predetermined feminist definition must be either rejected as un-Biblical or summarily explained away. Mostly, passages that teach a woman's role is to be one of subjection[18] are interpreted as

---

17 See Galatians 4:7.
18 For example, 1 Corinthians 11:3; 14:34; 1 Timothy 2:11; Ephesians 5:22; Colossians 3:18; 1 Peter 3:1.

culturally mandated and not suitable for all time. It is the teaching of those who hold this belief that the cultural submission of women taught in the aforementioned passages would eventually evolve into the total gender equality and role-interchangeability that they erroneously think Galatians 3:28 to be teaching. (Incidentally, I have had conversations with Christian women who have made this exact same argument.)

But Equality And Subordination Are Not Contradictions

The so-called "Biblical feminists" are wrong! *Equality and subordination are not contradictions.* The Bible teaches that, as divine image-bearers, the female and male are totally equal. Furthermore, the Bible teaches that the female is not a second-class citizen of the kingdom of God. It teaches, in fact, that she is totally equal in her access to the salvation that takes place in Christ.

At the same time, the Bible emphatically teaches that the female role is to be one of submission. Unless one is willing to charge the Holy Spirit with being inconsistent and contradictory (and what true Bible believer would ever think of doing such a thing?), then one is forced to conclude that subordination and equality are not contradictory. In order to make this point, I want to turn your attention to one irrefutable example: Jesus of Nazareth.

The Son of God's submission to His Heavenly Father stands as the conclusive example that equality and subordination are not contradictory.[19] The Bible teaches unequivocally that there never was a time when the Son of God ever ceased to be fully God.[20] Ontologically (i.e., having to do with His nature and being), the

---

[19] See 1 Corinthians 11:3 and 15:28.
[20] See Colossians 2:9.

second person of the Godhead was equal with His Father.[21] Even so, whenever the Bible says that God the Father sent His Son into the world,[22] it is understood that the Son's role was one of subordination: namely, the Father commands and sends; the Son obeys and comes. Only a heretic would be so bold as to suggest that the Son is a lesser God because it is His role to be submissive to His Father. In addition, the Bible tells us the Holy Spirit was sent by both the Father and the Son.[23] Does this mean that He was even a lesser God than the Son who was already a lesser God than His Father? Again, none but a heretic would teach such a thing.

If Christ's subjection to His Father does not suggest inferiority, then the wife's subjection to her husband certainly does not imply her inferiority, as feminists so wrongly insist. The difference between the Father, Son, and Holy Spirit is a *functional* one, not an *essential* one. They differ not in their essence or nature, but in the different roles they carry out in the Godhead. Similarly, men and women do not differ in their humanness, only in the roles they have been assigned by their Creator. Neither the natural equality that men and women enjoy as creatures made in the image of God nor their covenant equality in the kingdom of God is abrogated by the Biblical assignment of masculine and feminine roles.

Thus, as the Bible teaches us, the God-ordained role of the husband is to exercise a loving headship in the Home. The wife, that same Bible tells us, must willingly submit to her husband's rule. As co-regents, their children are required to obey them both. Thus, it is in the Home that men and women are first exposed to the obligations and responsibilities of delegated authority.

---

21 See Philippians 2:6.
22 In places like John 3:17, for example.
23 See John 14:26; 15:26; 16:7.

But What, If Any, Are The Limitations Of Such Authority?

Until we answer this question, our study of the Home has no value in our attempt to understand the relationship that exists between the Christian and the State. We will do this by understanding the limitations God has placed on the husband's exercise of authority and, as it relates to this, the wife's and children's obligations to submit to the husband's/father's authority.

As we've learned, the husband's authority is *delegated* authority, and all delegated authority, by definition, is subservient to the grantor of such authority. The Creator and Sustainer of the universe is the ultimate Grantor of any and all authority, as the Scriptures make clear.[24] This means that the husband's authority is limited to matters of expedience, which means, in turn, that his authority does not extend to matters on which God has already legislated in His divine revelation. This concept may not be clear at first, but it is imperative to understanding the limits of delegated authority. In other words, although the husband has been given the authority to rule the Home, such authority does not extend to altering or denigrating what God has taught in His word, whether through *command, example* or *necessary inference*. When the husband exercises himself to do so, he has stepped outside his realm of authority and those otherwise subject to him (viz., his wife and children) are not obligated to obey in such matters. Although such will be viewed as disobedience by those attempting to exercise such power, such disobedience, if it is even proper to call it this, is really "holy disobedience," which is just another way of identifying the godly disobedience our allegiance to God sometimes requires of us.

---

24 See footnotes 1 through 3 in this chapter for the Biblical references.

A Tragic Example

For example, a preacher who was there when it happened told me the sad story of a woman he baptized into Christ whose husband tried to prevent her from worshiping with the saints. He did most everything he could to make her life miserable. But because she understood, and was determined to honor, her obligation to obey the Lord concerning this matter, she was willing to disobey her husband in order to assemble and worship with the saints. In his rants, he even threatened to kill her if she continued to meet with the church. All can sympathize with this woman's plight. Nevertheless, she continued to assemble with her brethren. Even those who picked her up for services were subjected to verbal abuse and even likewise threatened.

One Lord's day the husband made good on his threatenings. As the preacher drove the woman home in his pickup truck with her child sitting next to her, the husband, upon their arrival, came out on the front porch and fired his rifle in their direction, hitting his wife in the head and killing her instantly. As soon as he did so, there was remorse. Therefore, he spared the preacher and the child. Nevertheless, the bitter deed was done and his wife was dead, and he, in his ungodly rage, had killed her.

How tragic, you are no doubt thinking. But while you're thinking, ask yourself this question: Did this woman bring this tragedy on herself by continuing to disobey her husband? Of course not!, you may be thinking. Well, then, if not, why not? In other words, doesn't the Bible teach that a wife is under obligation to obey her husband "in everything"? Furthermore, are not his children scripturally admonished to obey him "in all things"? Well, yes, you say, but the "all" and "everything" of such passages are "*superseded* by other passages that require one to obey God rather than man when man commands something that interferes with obeying the Lord." Well, you're on the right track and, consequently, almost right. However, "almost right" isn't good enough when it comes to properly understanding this most important of subjects, for in understanding this subject properly, one will come to understand that God never places us in the impossible position of having to violate one of His commands by obeying another. In other words, if one of God's laws can "supersede" another, this makes one of God's laws superior to another. Although this idea is all too common among Christians, it is not what the Bible says. I'll have more to say about this momentarily, but first we must spend some time with the Principle of Qualification.

The Principle Of Qualification

The ancients wisely declared, "*Scriptura scripturam interpretatur*," or "Scripture interprets Scripture." If the Bible is God's Word, then it stands to reason that it must not be inconsistent with itself. In point of fact, one divine Author, the Holy Spirit, inspired the entire Bible. Therefore, it is inconceivable it could contradict itself. An essential rule of Bible study, let's call it the *synthesis principle*, puts scripture together with scripture to arrive at clear, consistent meaning. In 2 Peter 1:19-21, Peter wrote:

> *We also have the prophetic word made more sure, which you do well to heed as a light that shines in a dark place, until the day dawns and the morning star rises in your hearts; knowing this first, that no prophecy of Scripture is of any private interpretation, for prophecy never came by the will of man, but holy men of God spoke as they were moved by the Holy Spirit.*

In other words, there is never any place in Bible study for, "To me, this passage means..." On the contrary, the Bible cannot have one meaning for *you* and another meaning for *me*. Whatever the Scriptures are saying, it is saying the same thing to both of us. Consequently, the best way to interpret the Bible is to let it interpret itself.

Thinking Of The Bible As A Symphony Orchestra

If the Bible is thought of as a symphony orchestra, and the Holy Spirit as the famed Arturo Toscanini, or some other great conductor, then just as the orchestra plays the notes the great conductor desires, so the Bible, with its great assortment of instruments, produces the message the Holy Spirit wants produced—remember, if you will, that "no prophecy of Scripture is of any private interpretation."[25] When synthesized, or put together, we have the entire symphony or word of God, as the case may be. Just as each instrumentalist's part becomes fully clear when played in relation to all the other parts, so any one passage of the Bible becomes clear only when compared to all other passages. This means that if we hold an interpretation of one passage that contradicts another, at least one of these passages is being interpreted incorrectly. The Holy Spirit does not—indeed, cannot—disagree with Himself. For example, one passage cannot be saying we are saved by faith alone[26] if there is another clear passage that says we are *not* saved by faith only.[27] Therefore, passages where the obvious meanings are clear help us to understand passages that are sometimes less clear. The wise Bible student is careful not to build a doctrine on a single obscure or unclear passage. Some otherwise intelligent men have done this to their own detriment.

---

[25] 1 Peter 1:20.
[26] See Romans 3:28.
[27] See James 2:24.

A Definition

Comparing Scripture with Scripture helps us to understand that one passage can actually amplify, clarify, modify, or qualify another. In this section, it is our responsibility to focus on something I'm calling the "qualification of Scripture." By *qualify*, it is meant that one passage can limit or restrict another. Although a qualification may appear at first to be a contradiction or denial of a particular scripture, it is not. A qualification merely sets the particular passage in perspective by applying additional information about the topic under discussion. As we shall see, a qualification may occur in the immediate, general, or remote context. Now stay with me on this, if you will, for it is very important to understand this principle if we are to ever unravel what some think to be contradictory passages having to do with submission to authority exercised in the Home, the State, and the Church.

The Immediate Context

Sometimes a qualification is found in the very passage itself. In Matthew 19:9, for example, the "except for sexual immorality" phrase qualifies, "And I say to you, whoever divorces his wife...and marries another, commits adultery; and whoever marries her who is divorced commits adultery." Without this exception clause (or qualification), divorcing one's mate and marrying another would always be wrong.

Another example is found in 1 Corinthians 5:9-10, where Paul writes:

> *I wrote to you in my epistle not to keep company with sexually immoral people. Yet I certainly did not mean with the sexually immoral people of this world, or with the covetous,*

or extortioners, or idolaters, since then you would need to go out of the world.

It should be easy to see that what Paul wrote in verse 10 immediately qualifies what he said in verse 9.

Yet another example is found in 1 Corinthians 10:23-33, where Paul mentions not doing some things "for conscience' sake."[28] It's not until we get to verse 29 that we hear him say: "Conscience, I say, not your own, but that of the other. For why is my liberty judged by another man's conscience?" Without this immediate qualification, we would not know that this passage was actually referring to another man's conscience, rather than our own.

In point of fact, immediate, clear-cut qualifications of Scripture are very rare. Imagine what the Bible would read like if, after every bit of instruction in the Bible, God would have explained what the passage did *not* mean. Such a list of seemingly endless qualifications would surely cause us to lose the crucial point under discussion. Even so, the principle of qualification is an extremely important concept to understand when trying to discover the correct meaning of any Bible passage.

However, the interpretation of a verse in its immediate context is actually the foundation of Bible interpretation and serves as a precedent for how the process should be employed in the larger context of Scripture. Therefore, understanding how the principle of qualification is to be employed, we are ready to examine some passages that are qualified by the general context.

---

[28] See verses 25, 27 and 28.

The General Context

An example of a qualification in the general context is Solomon's frequently misinterpreted statement, "The dead know nothing."[29] Solomon is not denying continuing existence or consciousness after one experiences physical death, as some think. This would be a clear contradiction of the necessary inference of Exodus 3:6, where God stated, "I am the God of your father—the God of Abraham, the God of Isaac, and the God of Jacob." The necessary inference, according to Jesus,[30] is that Abraham, Isaac, and Jacob, although physically dead, remain in a state of conscious existence. The Sadducees, of course, did not believe that a human being survived physical death.[31] Because they failed to make the necessary conclusion of Exodus 3:6, Jesus said, in Mark 12:27, that they were "greatly mistaken." One might suspect that the Sadducees may have even cited Ecclesiastes 9:5 as their proof-text. Yet, when we consider the story Jesus told of the rich man and Lazarus,[32] then we realize that Solomon's statement could not be referring to one's lack of consciousness beyond the grave.

There is, of course, the possibility that Solomon could have been mistaken about what he wrote, and that the Holy Spirit permitted his misunderstanding to be recorded in Scripture. This happens occasionally in Scripture. However, when one considers the surrounding context of Solomon's statement, this possibility is immediately eliminated. In the general context, it is clear that Solomon is referring to life "under the sun."[33] In fact, much of what

---

29 Ecclesiastes 9:5.
30 See Mark 12:18-27.
31 See Acts 23:8.
32 See Luke 16:19-31.
33 Ecclesiastes 9:3, 6, and 9.

Solomon says in this book should be viewed within the "under the sun" context. There are twenty-seven occurrences of the phrase "under the sun" in the book, beginning in Ecclesiastes 1:3 and ending in 10:5. Thus, Solomon's "the dead know nothing" statement is restricted or limited to an ongoing knowledge of the earthly affairs experienced by those who are still physically alive and, thus, does not extend to those who are dead but still alive in the spirit.

Another example of a general context qualification is found in 1 Corinthians 10:23, where the apostle Paul writes, "All things are lawful for me, but not all things are helpful; all things are lawful for me, but not all things edify." Some have wrongly taken this passage to mean that those in Christ are no longer subject to law. Although it is true that a Christian is not dependent upon a system of perfect law-keeping for justification, he is, nevertheless, under law to Christ.[34] Paul, who is speaking by inspiration, is not saying everything (e.g., fornication, adultery, lying, theft, *et cetera*, which are clearly condemned in other passages) is lawful, which would make the Scriptures contradictory. Instead, the general context indicates that what he's saying is that within the category of things that are lawful, there are some things that are not helpful or expedient. The context informs us that whatever the Christian does must glorify God (verse 31) and that even our liberty (viz., the "all things" that "are lawful") may be limited by another person's conscience (verses 27-29). In other words, even when something is lawful for me, I should usually refrain from doing it if it will give "offense either to the Jews or the Greeks or to the church of God" (verse 32). I say "usually," because even this doctrine is qualified.

For example, it is important to understand that Paul is not writing in this passage of things that are required. In other words,

---

[34] See 1 Corinthians 9:21 and Galatians 6:2.

if my devotion to Jesus Christ offends a Jew or Muslim, (e.g., invoking His name in prayer), then so be it—I must "obey God rather than men."[35] On the other hand, I will not offend my Muslim or Jewish dinner guest by serving him pork, which, as a Christian, I am at liberty to eat or not to eat. And, in the case under consideration in the passage, I need not be overly scrupulous about eating meat, whether selecting it in the market place or eating it when it is set before me at an unbeliever's table. But on the other hand, if I am informed that the meat has been sacrificed to an idol, which, in and of itself, does not affect the edibility of the meat, I must, nevertheless, refrain from eating it. This is done not to appease my own conscience, but so as not to embolden the conscience of another.

Furthermore, 1 Corinthians 10:23-33, along with 1 Corinthians 8:8-9, effectively qualify the commandment given elsewhere to "abstain from things offered to idols."[36] Actually, this last example is an illustration of a qualification that takes place in the remote context and, therefore, it is to this subject that we now turn our attention.

The Remote Context

In Matthew 19:26, Jesus says: "With men this is impossible, but with God all things are possible." When we contemplate God's omnipotence, this is exactly the idea we have in mind. In fact, if one were to ask a group of Christians to define God's omnipotence, they would probably answer that omnipotence means God

---

35 Acts 5:29.
36 Acts 15:29.

can do anything and everything. Even so, this is not what the Bible teaches!

In Hebrews 6:18, the Bible says "it is impossible for God to lie." This is not, as some suppose, a denial of the truth taught in Matthew 19:26. It is, instead, a qualification. God, who is holy, "cannot lie."[37] Consequently, we understand that what Jesus meant in Matthew 19:26 is "with God all things [that are consistent with His nature] are possible." So, the phrase "all things" does not always mean all things. The "all things" in one passage may very well be qualified by something said in another passage.

This brings us to Jacob's statement in Genesis 32:30, which says, "For I have seen God face to face, and my life is preserved." If what God told Moses in Exodus 33:20 is true, namely, "You cannot see My face; for no man shall see Me, and live," then Jacob's statement in Genesis 32:30 is problematic. Unfamiliar with the principle of qualification, some view Jacob's statement as a clear-cut contradiction of Genesis 32:20 and other passages,[38] ultimately reflecting on the integrity of the entire Bible. But if the Bible is what it claims to be, then it simply cannot be contradicting itself. How, then, can we resolve this apparent dilemma?

First of all, God "cannot lie."[39] So we can be sure that Jacob did not see the face of God in the same sense God uses this expression in Exodus 33:20. When one looks at the context of God's statement to Moses, it seems clear He uses "My face" to mean His pure Spirit essence, "dwelling in unapproachable light, whom no man has seen or can see."[40] Thus, Jacob cannot be understood to be saying he actually saw the pure and glorious Spirit essence of

---

37 Titus 1:2.
38 See John 1:18; 1 Timothy 6:16; and 1 John 4:12.
39 Titus 1:2.
40 1 Timothy 6:16.

Almighty God. If so, then Jacob was mistaken and his misperception was accurately recorded here like other false ideas and downright untruths that are cited elsewhere in Scripture.[41]

Second, when we consider what was said about this incident in Hosea 12:4, then it is clear that Jacob wrestled with a not so ordinary angel. In fact, when we examine verses 4 and 5, it appears Jacob wrestled with the Angel of Yahweh,[42] elsewhere called the Angel of God,[43] or the Angel of His Presence,[44] who some believe to be pre-incarnate appearances of the Lord Himself. Others who encountered this unique Angel had very similar reactions.[45] On these occasions God evidently took upon Himself human form for the express purpose of manifesting Himself to those involved. In theological parlance, these manifestations are called theophanies, which means "appearances of God." Because those who saw God in these theophanies did not see God in His true Spirit essence, they did not die, as they had expected. This interpretation is compatible with all the accepted rules of Bible interpretation. As such, it is consistent with the totality of Scripture and it completely harmonizes what would otherwise be absolutely contradictory passages.

Finally, it is very important to see the Lord's unqualified endorsement of the Principle of Qualification. In his temptation of Jesus, Satan, according to 2 Peter 3:16, "twisted" the Scriptures by neglecting the principle of qualification. In Matthew 4:5-7, the Bible says:

---

41 For example, Satan's original lie is recorded in Genesis 3:4, as are the false theological ideas expressed by Job's friends.
42 See Exodus 3:2 and Judges 2:1.
43 See Exodus 14:19.
44 See Isaiah 63:9.
45 See Judges 6:22 and 13:22.

> *Then the devil took Him up into the holy city, set Him on the pinnacle of the temple, and said to Him, "If You are the Son of God, throw Yourself down. For it is written: 'He shall give His angels charge over you,' and, 'In their hands they shall bear you up, Lest you dash your foot against a stone.' Jesus said to him, "It is written again, 'You shall not tempt the LORD your God.'"*

Satan's citation of Psalm 91:11-12 was accurate but misapplied, in that the providential care promised in this passage did not include the deliberate testing of God's faithfulness. Jesus makes this clear in His citation of Deuteronomy 6:16, which says, "You shall not tempt the LORD your God." This means that Jesus gave His un-qualified endorsement to the Principle of Qualification when He made it clear that the protection offered in Psalm 91:11-12 is quali-fied by the Scriptures' teaching on man's obligation not to tempt God. In other words, being a child of God is not a license to act im-prudently or recklessly. Which is just another way of saying: If you can't swim, don't jump into water over your head to discover (i.e., to test) if God will save you.

So, What Does All This Have To Do With The Issue At Hand?

When we factor into our thinking the Principle of Qualifica-tion, it is not difficult to understand that the "everything" and "all things" of the husband's and father's authority are qualified by principles taught elsewhere in God's word. Consequently these passages were never intended to impinge upon territory belonging solely to God, but are, in fact, qualified by such things. Thus, pas-sages that say wives are to submit to their husbands "as is fitting in the Lord"[46] and that children are to obey their parents "in the Lord"[47] are examples of precisely this kind of qualification. We can be sure, then, that when God commanded wives to obey their husbands "in everything," He was speaking *only* of those things which fell within the husband's delegated authority.

Remember, man's delegated authority *only* applies to matters of expediency. This means that those areas where God has already legislated are off limits. So, when children are commanded to obey their parents "in the Lord," this *only* refers to those things that fall within the parents' delegated authority, nothing else. If a man functioning either as a husband or a parent commanded one under his authority to do something inconsistent with God's word, the one being so commanded would not be under any obligation to submit, as God never requires us to obey an unlawful command.[48]

Consequently, the obeying-God-rather-than-man principle espoused in Acts 4:19 and 5:29, although not referring to the Home, *per se*, is precisely the principle under discussion. In other words, no man invested by God with any kind of authority has the right to command anyone under his authority to do anything inconsistent with what God has said in His word. Things that are either commanded or prohibited by God cannot be interfered with by the exercise of delegated authority. This means there may well be times when a wife or a child is required by God to be disobedient to those who, under other circumstances, he or she would be

[46] Colossians 3:18.

[47] Ephesians 6:1.

[48] In this regard, it is interesting to note that the *Uniform Code of Military Justice*, which governs all military personnel serving the United States of America, extends to every serviceman and servicewoman the right to resist and, if necessary, to disobey any and all unlawful commands issued by a superior, up to and including the President of the United States, whose authority, of course, makes him the military's Commander-in-Chief.

obligated to obey. And when this happens, no guilt attaches to either the wife or the child.

Now, it needs to be pointed out just here that nothing said so far has anything to do with the so-called higher-lower law distinction that some try to make. For if God had actually implemented a higher-lower structure of law, as some contend, such would ultimately require us to disobey His lesser commands in order to obey the greater ones. But this, after everything is said and done, would make every one of us lawbreakers and, therefore, partakers of unrighteousness. What's more, and just think about this for a moment, this would all be at God's command. Who can believe it?

In truth, the Bible teaches no such doctrine. But you may be thinking, "Doesn't Jesus, Himself, talk about 'the weightier matters of the law'?"[49] Yes, He most certainly does, but what He says is not that one can break a lower law in order to obey a higher one. No, no, a thousand times, no!

In the very context in which Jesus speaks of the weightier matters of the law, He says, "These you ought to have done *without leaving the others undone*" (emphasis mine-AT). He's not saying the lesser matters of the law can be overlooked, and therefore violated, in order to obey the weightier ones, as the higher-lower law proponents claim. Instead, He's saying that within the grand scheme of things there are some principles "more important" (this is the way some versions render the Greek word translated "weightier") to understand—things like doing justice, loving mercy, and walking humbly with God.[50] Such principles, Jesus claims, sum up every requirement to be found in God's law.

---

49 Matthew 23:23.
50 See Micah 6:8.

In yet another place, this same point is summed up in one word: Love, which is, we are told by an apostle of Christ, "the fulfilling of the law."[51] The following episode, which is recorded in Matthew 22:34-40, deals with the two very different perspectives placed on this word:

> *But when the Pharisees heard He had silenced the Sadducees, they gathered together. Then one of them, a lawyer, asked Him a question, testing Him, and saying, "Teacher, which is the great commandment in the law?" Jesus said to him, "You shall love the Lord your God with all your heart, with all your soul, and with all your mind.' And the second is like it: 'You shall love your neighbor as yourself.' On these two commandments hang all the Law and the Prophets." [52]*

In other words, "against such [Love] there is no law,"[53] for all such Love is, ultimately, the "fulfilling of the law."[54]

Some Final Thoughts On The Home

In concluding this rather lengthy examination of the Home, we do so with the understanding that there are limitations placed on the God-ordained authority exercised within it. Those in submissive roles (the wife and children) should realize they are not under obligation to follow the commands of the husband/father if they would cause them to violate the will of God. In other words, absolutely no breaking of one's obligation to submit to one with delegated authority occurs in these situations and circumstances

---

51 Romans 10:13.
52 Jesus is using Deuteronomy 6:5 as His quoted text here.
53 Galatians 5:22-23.
54 Romans 13:10.

precisely because those scriptures requiring submission to delegated authority are not applicable in such cases.

We were helped in this by our exposure to the Principle of Qualification, which teaches us that one passage can actually amplify, clarify, modify, or qualify another. But in understanding this truth, it is important to recognize that any such qualification of delegated authority is not based on the argument that duties commanded by God, like not forsaking the assembling of the saints,[55] take precedent over duties commanded by man (e.g., "I forbid you to worship with that church"). Instead, it is qualified by the truth that submission to delegated authority only applies to matters of expedience, which means that a husband or parent has no right (i.e., authority) to contest any item of divine legislation.

Remember here the case of the woman mentioned earlier who was killed by her husband after returning from assembling with the saints on the Lord's day. Yes, she was certainly under obligation to obey her husband "in everything," as the Scriptures require, but this "everything" is clearly qualified/limited by the God-given obligation to assemble with the saints on the Lord's day. Therefore, one can be sure that one of God's laws which is presently in force will never supersede another of His laws currently in force.

As was pointed out at the beginning of this chapter, understanding the exercise and limitations of delegated authority in the Home, the very first of God's divine institutions, will ultimately aid us in understanding the thorny issues associated with the Christian's obligation to obey the State. With this said, we must now turn our attention to the Church, a very special, God-ordained institution that followed the establishment of the State by a

---

[55] Hebrews 10:25.

considerable length of time and, when properly understood, serves to reinforce the lessons on delegated authority we have already learned.

The Church

Because congregations of the Lord's people are composed of Christians working together for a common cause, God has ordained a structure of authority (government) within each congregation. By examining the nature and limits of such authority, one comes to further appreciate the limits that are always placed on the exercise of delegated authority and will, in the end, be better able to understand the limits God has placed on the State's authority.

To begin with, Jesus Christ established only one church (sometimes referred to as a "body") of which He, and He alone, is the Head. This is made clear in Ephesians 1:22-23, Ephesians 4:4, and Colossians 1:18. Consequently, "the man Christ Jesus,"[56] and this refers to the ascended and glorified Jesus, functions as this body's High Priest and only Mediator.[57] Thus, the church belonging to Christ needs no earthly mediator through which it offers its sacrifices, and any such provisional system is a perversion of the "My church" of Matthew 16:18. As such, the one and only true catholic church (i.e., the universal body of believers) has no earthly head or organizational structure. This means that all ecclesiastical constructions, whether they be Catholic or Protestant, are not just extra-biblical, but anti-biblical as well. "In Him,"[58] and this is to say "in connection with" Jesus Christ, the church is complete, and

---

[56] 1 Timothy 2:5.
[57] For a further exploration of this subject, please refer to the book of Hebrews.
[58] Colossians 2:10.

because it is, it needs no exalted priestly caste, like the old Jewish system, to intercede or mediate on its behalf.

Nevertheless, the Lord instructed His "called out" group of people[59] (i.e., His church) to organize themselves into local congregations. Such were referred to as "churches of Christ,"[60] along with other scriptural designations. Consequently, within the pages of the New Testament, we can read about the church at Corinth,[61] the churches of Galatia,[62] the saints that made up the church at Ephesus,[63] Philippi,[64] and Colosse.[65] We can further read of churches at Smyrna, Pergamos, Thyatira, Sardis, Philadelphia and Laodicea.[66] According to 1 Peter 5:1-5, the men in these local congregations who had the "oversight" (the Greek word here is *episkopeo*, from which we derive the word *bishop*), were also called "elders." The English word *elders* is translated from the Greek *presbuteros*, which in a transliterated form is "presbyter." Thus, an elder (or presbyter) was a bishop (i.e., one who exercised oversight) in a local congregation. This is borne out by the immediate passage under consideration, and by others, like 1 Timothy 3:1-7 and Titus 1:5-9, where the qualifications of these men are specifically enumerated.

In Paul's letter to Timothy, he calls these uniquely qualified men "bishops." Then in Titus he refers to the same group of men as not just bishops, but also "elders." Consequently, the Scriptures

---

59 The English word "church" comes from the Greek word *ekklesia*, which means a called out gathering or assembly.
60 Romans 16:16.
61 See 1 Corinthians 1:2.
62 See Galatians 1:2.
63 See Ephesians 1:1.
64 See Philippians 1:1.
65 See Colossians 1:2.
66 See Revelation 2-3.

make it clear that those who served as elders and bishops in local churches of Christ were not men with different offices (or functions); but were, instead, men who were being referred to by terms that either described their *maturity* (they were elders or older men) or *oversight* (or bishopric). Then, in Peter's instructions in 1 Peter 5:2, we learn that these very same men were to "feed" the flock of God which was among them. The NKJV translates this word as "shepherd," while the ASV says "tend." The Greek word so translated is *poimaino*, from which we get the word "pastor." So, according to the New Testament, the terms *elder*, *bishop* and *pastor* are used interchangeably of the same man, and are not titles *per se*. Instead, they simply serve to describe *who* and *what* these men are in connection with the "flock," or local church, of which they are members. (It is worth noting here that it was only after some began changing the government of the local church, mimicking the Greek-Roman culture in which they lived, that they developed an ecclesiastical order that conferred a higher ranking on a bishop than they did an elder, eventually granting to bishops oversight over more than the local church of which they were a member.)

In addition, the bishops/elders/pastors who exercised the oversight of local churches of Christ were *always* referred to in the Scriptures in the plural. For example, when Paul was in Miletus and wanted to speak with the leaders of the Ephesian church, he sent for "the elders [plural] of the church."[67] This will not surprise the careful Bible student, for in Acts 14:23 Paul and Barnabas, in their second missionary journey, had "appointed elders [plural] in every church." Further, in a letter written to Christians everywhere, James assumes the established order in every church would be "elders" (again, plural), for he instructed Christians, no matter

---

67 Acts 20:17.

where they were, to "call for the elders [plural] of the church."[68]
One must conclude, then, that the New Testament order was that
if a local church was blessed to have elders,[69] there would always be
at least two of them. Thus, a local church that was scripturally and
fully organized had a plurality of elders/bishops/pastors who exercised oversight in that church. They had to meet certain stringent
qualifications[70] and be selected by the church of which they were
members.[71] Thus, one-man rule of a local congregation would
never occur if Scripture was being followed.

As noted previously, Genesis 1:27 makes it clear that both
men and women equally bear the divine image and are, therefore,
absolutely equal when it comes to their relationship with God and
one another and are, as a result, joint "heirs together of the grace of
life."[72] At the same time, God created different roles for men and
women in the Home, and as we shall see, this is true for the
Church as well, as it is men, not women, who have the oversight of
the local congregation. This does not mean that women are not
called upon to be leaders in the Church, any more than they are
not scripturally prohibited from leading in their homes, only that
men within both these venues exercise the primary leadership.
Thus, there should be no doubt in the Christian's mind that the
primary role of oversight in the Church, like the Home, is male.

Because the Church is a family of sorts (albeit a rather extended family, according to Ephesians 3:15) that cries, according to
Romans 8:16-17, "Abba, Father," we should not be surprised that

---

68 James 5:14.
69 This was not a given, for there would *not* always be men with the
necessary qualifications.
70 See 1 Timothy 3; Titus 1.
71 See Acts 6:3.
72 1 Peter 3:7.

primary leadership in the local church (which is, in turn, usually made up of several, if not many, individual families) is the prerogative of not just one man, but a plurality of men who meet the qualifications laid out in 1 Timothy 3 and Titus 1. Thus, the God-ordained eldership of the local church will always consist of a plurality of men who have first proven themselves successful leaders in their own homes—men who have, thankfully, already exhibited loving, gentle and considerate oversight of their wives and children.[73] We ought to praise God for His magnificent gifts to the church.[74]

Because elders/pastors/bishops are commanded to lead by example, according to 1 Peter 5:3, some have thought that their oversight does not entail an actual "rule." These folks are wrong. The Bible says unequivocally that these men do exercise "rule" in the local church.[75] The word translated "rule" in the Timothy references is *proistemi*, which carries with it the idea of "standing before" and "presiding," according to *Strong's*, and to "be over" and "superintend," according to *Thayer*. In the Hebrews references, the Greek word translated "rule" is *hegeomai*, and is defined by both *Thayer* and *Strong's* as "to lead, rule, command, have authority over." So, it can be seen that "government" at the hands of elders/bishops/pastors is what God desires for churches of Christ, and in exercising this governance or "piloting," as this is one of the meanings of the word according to *Strong's*, they exercise a "rule" in the local church that will be obeyed by every submissive member.[76] (In further explanation of this, compare 1 Corinthians 12:28,

---

[73] See Ephesians 5:2ff. and 1 Peter 3:7.

[74] See Ephesians 4:7-16 and notice that "pastors" are specifically mentioned in verse 11b.

[75] See 1 Timothy 3:5; 5:17; Hebrews 13:7, 17 and 24.

[76] See Hebrews 13:17.

where it is recorded that God gives "governments" as a gift to churches, with Ephesians 4:11, where it is said that the ascended Christ gives "pastors" to aid in the perfecting of the saints, and then factor in to all this the idea that these passages are referring to the work of elders as they govern the flock which is among them.)

Even so, the Bible makes it clear that the *rule* of such men does not partake of the characteristics so prevalent in the world, which consist of controlling, lording it over, and domineering those who are deemed to be in subjection to them.[77] This means that the leadership of elders, who see themselves, ultimately, as humble servants of the Lord, does not ask of others things they are not willing to do themselves. As such, they will always be serving as "examples to the flock."

But none of this means, as some claim, that the elders' rule is actualized *only* through example. Instead, members of the local church are commanded to, "Obey those who rule over you, and be submissive, for they watch out for your souls, as those who must give account."[78] The Hebrew writer continues, "Let them do so with joy and not with grief, for that would be unprofitable for you."[79] The "joy" of Hebrews 13:17b refers to what the elders would experience as the result of the congregation's willing submission and obedience to their rule. But if there was "grief," which would be an obvious indication that those in the elders' charge were, in fact, being disobedient, then such would not be "profitable" for them. Why? Because God, no doubt, would be provoked by such groanings to exact judgment on the disobedient. In other

---

[77] See 1 Peter 5:3, where elders are told their rule is not to be as "lords over," as the Gentiles rule (cf. Mark 10:42 and Luke 22:24-27), but as "examples."

[78] Hebrews 13:17a.

[79] Hebrews 13:17b.

words, if elders must give an account to the Lord for their watch-care over the church, then it stands to reason that any rebellion against their authority would be speedily and appropriately judged by the Lord. Furthermore, if such became necessary, it would definitely not be profitable for the rebels, for the grief they cause will be justly recompensed by the grief they receive.[80]

Consequently, the idea that elders do not exercise actual authority in the local church, *only* leading by their examples, is an idea that is absolutely foreign to the New Testament. Elders do, in fact, exercise God-given authority in the local church, and those who are the rightful subjects of such authority, in order to be pleasing to the Lord, must be willing to submit to such authority.

So, with this said, it is time for us to consider those situations where "holy disobedience" would be necessary.

The Limits Of Elders' Authority

Just like in the Home, there are limits to the authority men are to exercise over the Church. Although members of a congregation, individually and collectively, are under divine obligation to submit to their elders, the rule of such men, like that which the husband exercises in the Home, is only legitimate in matters of expedience. For in those areas where God has already legislated, elders must not, indeed cannot, tread.

For example, meeting together on the first day of the week to partake of the Lord's supper is something the New Testament teaches Christians are obligated to do. It does so through a direct statement, an approved example, and a necessary inference. These are found in 1 Corinthians 11:23-26 and Acts 20:7. In the first

---

[80] See also 2 Thessalonians 1:4-6.

passage, we are confronted with a commandment (i.e., a direct statement) that we are, as often as we partake of the Lord's supper, to do so in remembrance of our Lord. Then, in the second passage, we are confronted with an approved example (specifically, an approved, apostolic example) of a congregation of the Lord's people coming together on the first day of the week to eat the Lord's supper. Finally, in the same passage, we necessarily infer that this commemoration is to be done each and every first day of the week.

So, how does this relate to elders and their authority? Well, consistent with their understanding of the particular circumstances that exist in their congregation (e.g., the work schedules and time constraints of those who make up the church), elders have the authority to decide exactly *when* on the first day of the week it is most expedient for them to meet. Consistent with the admonition not to exercise themselves "as being lords," *vis-à-vis* 1 Peter 5:3, one can be sure that such a decision would never be made by a set of godly elders in an arbitrary or self-serving way. Several factors might come into play regarding the final decision of when to meet, but foremost would certainly be what is best (i.e., the most expedient) for the congregation as a whole. It is exactly this kind of authority that has been delegated by God to elders, and it is exactly this kind of authority members of the congregation are required to obey. However, elders have absolutely no authority to change the day the congregation meets to partake of the Lord's supper, just as they have no authority to prescribe other elements to be used in the Lord's supper, as these have already been specified in Matthew 26:17-29—namely, "unleavened bread" and "fruit of the vine."

There are other things we could talk about along these lines, but I think this simple example demonstrates that the elders' authority is limited to matters of expedience and nothing else. Consequently, elders, like husbands in the Home, must be very careful not to develop a haughty, self-absorbed, domineering spirit, which would be nothing less than sinful. Finally, it almost goes without saying that such a spirit would make life in the Home or Church most miserable.

Therefore, elders have been delegated by God to make decisions involving the work of the Church; but in the exercise of such authority, they have no jurisdiction in the Home, as such is something that belongs primarily to the husband/father. If, of course, it should come to the attention of the elders that a husband/father who is a member of the congregation was conducting himself sinfully in the exercise of his headship, the elders would certainly have the authority to rebuke such behavior, calling upon the guilty husband/father to repent. If, per chance, he refused to do so, it would then be a matter for the whole church, according to Matthew 18:17. If he still refused to repent, the elders would have no choice but to lead the church in withdrawing from the offender.[81] Thus, there may be times when there seems to be an overlapping between authority exercised in the Home and Church. However, such is only an allusion. Elders, even when taking the action mentioned above, exercise no authority in the Home. Instead, they are simply exercising the responsibility and authority commanded them by God, who demands that elders watch for the souls of those in their charge.[82]

Examining, then, the exercise of delegated authority both in the Home and the Church, as we have, and realizing there are always limitations placed on the exercise of such authority, we are now ready to examine the scope of the State's authority.

---

81 2 Thessalonians 3:6 and 1 Corinthians 5:11-13.
82 Hebrews 13:17.

The State

The earliest reference in Scripture to the authority of the State is inferred from Genesis 9:6, which says, "Whoever sheds man's blood, by man his blood shall be shed; for in the image of God He made man." Enlightened people down through the ages have recognized this principle as the very foundation of civilized society. Because man is uniquely made in the image of his Creator, his "right to life" must not be interfered with by any other creature. This is made clear by what was previously said in verse 5. Thus, if this principle or law is broken and a man is murdered, then the murderer must be put to death, as this is the clear, unequivocal teaching of these verses. Furthermore, it must be understood that this precept or principle was instituted prior to the Law of Moses given at Sinai, which was not until a much later date. Consequently, Genesis 9:6 has no more been rescinded than the fact that man is made in the image of God, for as long as the latter is true, the former will be in force.

Now, although it is true that the particular judicial process by which this is to be carried out is not specified in this verse, it is clear, nevertheless, that capital punishment is command by it. As H.C. Leupold, that great commentator on the book of Genesis, observed:

> *This verse attaches itself directly to the preceding, particularly to that part which says: "from man will I demand the soul of man."* [Of this previous verse, he said: "When man's blood is shed ruthlessly, without warrant and authority, there God Himself shall demand an account. He may do this by prompting human agents to punish the evildoer, or He may achieve His ends by ultimately exacting vengeance upon the murderer who has not been

brought to justice by man."] *This verse now shows how God does this demanding: He lets man be the avenger. As Luther already very clearly saw, by this word government is instituted, this basic institution for the welfare of man. For if man receives power over other men's lives under certain circumstances, then by virtue of having received power over the highest good that man has, power over the lesser things is naturally included, such as power over property to the extent of being able to exact taxes, over our persons to the extent of being able to demand various types of work and service, as need may arise. Government, then, being ground on this word, is not by human contract, or by surrender of certain powers, or by encroachment of priestcraft. It is a divine institution.*[83]

I agree with these observations. But that it is specifically the State that has been given delegated authority to punish, and even execute, criminals is made much clearer in the New Testament. In Romans 13:1, the apostle Paul said: "Let every soul be subject to the governing authorities. For there is no authority except from God, and the authorities that exist are appointed by God." Then to an evangelist, he wrote, "Remind them to be subject to rulers and authorities, to obey, to be ready for every good work."[84] Addressing this same issue, the apostle Peter said, "Therefore submit yourselves to every ordinance of man for the Lord's sake, whether to the king as supreme, or to governors, as to those who are sent by him for the punishment of evildoers and for the praise of those who do good."[85] In this regard, it should be noticed that Jesus, when standing before the Roman prefect (or procurator) Pontius

---

[83] *Exposition of Genesis*, Vol. 1, 1942, page 333.
[84] Titus 3:1.
[85] 1 Peter 2:13-14.

Pilate, did not deny that the governor had the power to rule the province of Judea, but instructed him that such authority derived ultimately from God. I'm fairly certain that Pilate had no real appreciation for what Jesus said, probably thinking he derived his power, instead, solely from Tiberius Caesar Augustus, who ruled Rome at that time. Jesus' point, of course, did not deal so much with Pilate's power over Him as much as it properly identified the source of Caesar's lawful authority. In Matthew 22:21, Jesus had already said about such authority that the Jews were obligated to "Render therefore to Caesar the things that are Caesar's, and to God the things that are God's." Although I think some have clearly invested the State with too much authority based upon their understanding of this passage, it should be clear that worship of Caesar as a god is something that could not be rendered by anyone being obedient to Jesus' words. However, that Caesar was invested with certain lawful authority cannot be doubted. Just what this entails is the subject of this book. It cannot be denied, then, that (1) the State, and the idea here is not any particular state, but the State in general, has been delegated by God to exercise authority and (2) as it does so, it is to be willingly obeyed:

> *Therefore submit yourselves to every ordinance of man for the Lord's sake, whether to the king as supreme, or to governors, as to those who are sent by him for the punishment of evildoers and for the praise of those who do good. For this is the will of God, that by doing good you may put to silence the ignorance of foolish men—as free, yet not using your liberty as a cloak for vice, but as servants of God. Honor all people. Love the brotherhood. Fear God. Honor the king.*[86]

---

[86] 1 Peter 2:13-17.

As we have already observed in the Home and the Church, delegated authority, although extremely important, always has limits. This is no less true when it comes to the State. Although the passage cited above makes it clear that we must be willing to submit "to every ordinance of man," we should know by now that such a statement is qualified and, therefore, refers *only* to those things that fall within the State's jurisdiction.

For example, the New Testament depicts the Church and the State as separate entities,[87] both of which are accountable to Him who has been given "all authority...in heaven and on earth" by His Father.[88] For not only is Jesus the "head of the church,"[89] but as the book of Revelation points out, He is also the "ruler of the kings of the earth."[90] Therefore, both Church and State must respect God's authority, upholding Righteousness and Justice in the process. Failure to do so results in the removal of the candlestick for the Church[91] and a rod of iron for the State.[92] Although it is true that under the Old Testament the kingdom of Israel was a theocracy (i.e., a combination of Church and State), under the New Testament, there is to be a separation of these two institutions.

Rendering To Caesar The Things That Are Caesar's, And To God The Things That Are God's

In 2 Corinthians 10:3-5, the role of the Church under Christ is presented as one of spiritual warfare. On the other hand, Caesar

---

[87] See Matthew 22:17-21.
[88] Matthew 28:18.
[89] Ephesians 1:22; Colossians 1:18.
[90] Revelation 1:5.
[91] See Revelation 2:5.
[92] See Revelation 12:5.

(i.e., the State) is given a physical sword (i.e., the penalty of death) to aid in its warfare against evildoers, according to Romans 13:4. Unlike Israel of old, the Church today is not in the business of taking human life. On the contrary, this is today the sole prerogative of the State.[93] But in doing so, the State is not free to arbitrarily and capriciously exercise itself, but must do so consistent with the principles of Righteousness and Justice taught in the Bible.

The government is, therefore, duty bound to protect the law-abiding and punish the evildoers. If a government consistently fails to meet its obligation "under God," and this would be evidence of a Revelation 13 government,[94] then there can be no real Justice. Under such government, the law-abiding become prey, not just evildoers. When this happens, society eventually experiences the fiery wrath of the Lord's righteous indignation, which ultimately manifests itself in some sort of judgment.

Thus, it is the responsibility of the Christian to be praying for the State that it will meet its obligation to maintain order in society.[95] In addition, the Christian will dutifully pay his taxes to support the State, and he will always be found obeying the laws of the land as long as these laws do not constitute a contravening of God's Word. But, and this is most important, the State has no authority to tell the Church what to do in spiritual matters. It cannot (i.e., "under God") tell the Church when, or when not, to pray; when to preach or not to preach; when to worship or not to worship. In these matters, the Church is amenable *only* to Christ. In purely secular matters, the Church belonging to Christ is obligated to respect

---

[93] See Romans 13:1-7.

[94] A Revelation 13 government is one that has fallen under the sway of Satan and is contrasted with the kind of government outlined in Romans 13, which is clearly a God-ordained government.

[95] See 1 Timothy 2:1-2.

and obey the laws of the land. This is, however, as far as it goes, and if, and when, the State seeks to regulate the Church spiritually, the Church is obligated to engage in holy disobedience.[96] Please understand that I am not talking hypotheticals here, as I have lived under the jurisdiction of just such a State and know of others around the world who presently live under such governments.

The Church is "the pillar and ground of the truth," according to 1 Timothy 3:15, and must preach the truth *whenever, wherever,* and *to whomever* it applies. It must do this without respect of persons. This may involve telling Caesar he is wrong on some moral or spiritual issue or that he has overstepped the bounds of his jurisdiction by trying to deal with those things that belong solely to the Church. The Truth must always be preached without fear or favor, not "having men's persons in admiration because of advantage," as Jude 16 puts it.

Yes, the Church is separate from the State, as these two God-ordained entities have two very separate roles—one spiritual and the other physical. And no matter what it may think, the State is not unaccountable to the Lord's principles of Righteousness and Justice. After all, it is subject to Christ and will answer to His "rod of iron" if its policies are contrary to His principles. In addition, the degree to which a particular government finds such things offensive is a good indicator of just how far down the path toward a Revelation 13 government it has traveled. We must not forget that the Bible says, "The wicked shall be turned into hell, and all the nations that forget God."[97]

---

96 See Acts 5:29.
97 Psalm 9:17.

In Conclusion

The Home, the Church, and the State have all been delegated authority in their realms of jurisdiction. Within either one of these realms, the other two have not been given any authority. Although this is an accurate depiction of these very different jurisdictions, it is, after everything is said and done, an oversimplification, for such does not address the various moral complexities that come into play as these three realms of jurisdiction attempt to function in a world that is, unfortunately, stained with and distorted by sin—a sinfulness that prods men and women to bite and devour one another in their ungodly pursuit of controlling, manipulative and self-serving power.

I like the way Kerry Duke deals with this in his informative and challenging little book, *Ox In The Ditch: Bible Interpretation as the Foundation of Christian Ethics.* In a chapter entitled "Qualification in Realms of Delegated Authority," he says:

> *Delegated authority, then, is qualified in a vertical direction by the revealed will of God in Scripture. It is also qualified in a horizontal direction because of the relationship between the different realms in which it resides. The home, the church, and civil government each have been delegated decision-making power in their respective realms of function. Parents have authority over their own children but not over children as a whole in society. Elders make decisions connected with the life and work of the church, but they have no such authority about the internal affairs of the homes of which Christians are also members. Ideally, civil government maintains order and peace in society as a whole without usurping the role of either the home or the church. Of course, the relationship between these realms has been*

*simplified; the moral complexities associated with govern-
ment intrusions into private matters are too numerous to dis-
cuss here. However, the fact remains that a separateness is to
exist between these realms of delegated authority. Otherwise,
biblical injunctions regarding submission in separate areas
are meaningless. Even more important is the fact that an understanding of the distinction between realms provides a general framework for evaluating different decisions.*[98]

In the next paragraph, he concluded by saying:

*The principle of submission to delegated authority gener-
ates a disposition that is foundational to Christianity: the re-
nouncing of one's own will to follow the will of another. The
duty to obey those in positions of authority is a responsibility
to God, so that in obeying or disobeying these people one is
obeying or disobeying God. It is also true that submission to
certain persons on earth is broadly analogous to subjection to
the Lord Himself. In terms of practical importance, however,
the principle of submission creates a humble attitude of obedience so basic in pleasing God, an attitude often described in
the Bible as the heart of a child (Matt. 18:1-4; I Cor. 14:20).*[99]

So, with this said, and having now some appreciation of both
the obligations *and* complexities associated with the exercise of
delegated authority, whether it be in the Home, the Church, or the
State, it is time to turn our attention to making sure we understand
the difference between "a right" and "a privilege."

---

[98] 1993, pages 84-85.
[99] Kerry, page 84

Chapter 2

Exploring The Difference Between "A Right" And "A Privilege": A Closer Look At This Nation's Founding Documents

I n the founding document of this nation, the Founding Fathers set forth their theory of rights with these words:

We hold these truths to be self-evident: that all men are created equal; that they are endowed by their Creator, with certain unalienable rights; that among these are life, liberty, and the pursuit of happiness.[1]

Aware they could no longer depend upon their "rights as Englishmen" before King George III (1760-1820) and Parliament, they appealed to that Law above all laws, which they believed granted to them certain "unalienable rights," namely, "life, liberty, and the pursuit of happiness." These, they believed, had been granted by "their Creator," who they understood to be higher than the think-sos of the king or the political machinations of Parliament. Whether the English authorities acknowledged such rights was

---

1 *The Declaration of Independence*, July 4, 1776. The full document has been reproduced in Appendix A. If you have never read it in its entirety, I hope you will take the time to do so.

totally irrelevant because such were "self-evident" (i.e., intuitively clear and certain). Such a theory of rights was highly evolved and manifested a comprehensive theological/ideological system of beliefs about God, Man, Nature, and Justice.

It is unfortunate, but true, that twenty-first-century society has lost its footing concerning such "rights," for too few remain who really believe such rights to be God-given. Most see rights only as something derived from the State (viz., the government giveth and the government taketh away). Although there may be much talk these days about "human rights," "civil rights," and even "animal rights," hardly anyone speaks of "unalienable rights." Commenting on this in his excellent little book on the religious significance of *The Declaration of Independence*, Gary T. Amos wrote:

> *America was founded on "unalienable rights"—those that a man may not unconditionally sell, trade, barter, or transfer without denying the image of God in himself. God the Creator endows man with these rights, annexing them to the human person. They are inalienable. For to deny these rights in a man is to deny that he is a human being.*[2]

As a creature made in the image of God, man has certain God-given rights that cannot be infringed upon or abridged by any other man, group, organization, or institution, and this certainly includes the State. Nevertheless, secularists and others of their ilk, who actively and variously promote the idolization of the State, along with the idolized State itself, do not take kindly to those who

---

[2] Gary T. Amos, *Defending The Declaration: How the Bible and Christianity Influenced the Writing of the Declaration of Independence*, 1989, page 104.

resist their idolatrous ways. As such a system becomes more and more institutionalized, and it is all too quickly becoming just that, Christians will find themselves in conflict with the State due to its ever widening influence. As the modern State becomes more and more pervasive, there is hardly anywhere it does not seek to exert itself. Conversely, a government that knows its God-given place is a government that's quite limited. Such will see itself as prohibited from interfering with God-given ("unalienable") rights. That this was unquestionably true of the American government is evidenced by *The Declaration of Independence* and subsequently *The Constitution of the United States of America*, both of which made it very clear that the new republic was a limited government, a government that would be most careful not to trample on the God-given rights of its citizens; a government that would, instead, conscientiously and vigorously defend these rights.

Governments, like men, are never perfect, but that ours at its beginning was attempting to be a Romans 13 government, and not a Revelation 13 one, is clear to the unprejudiced mind. As we've seen, the Declaration was religious at its very core. Even the Constitution, which is a very secular document (and rightly so, for it is, after all, a document designed to direct the civil government), in its very first amendment, said very clearly, "Congress shall make no law respecting an establishment of religion, or prohibiting the free exercise thereof; or abridging the freedom of speech, or of the press; or the right of the people peaceably to assemble, and to petition the government for a redress of grievances." There were nine other amendments that were ratified by three quarters of the delegates present, and these have come down to us as "The Bill of Rights." The ninth of these said, "The enumeration in the Constitution, of certain rights, shall not be construed to deny or disparage others retained by the people."

As I said, one would have to ignore the fact that our government was, at its inception, a limited government that recognized the Law above the law principle taught in God's word, a principle addressed numerous times in this study and says that all man-made law is amenable to God's law. Nevertheless, there are those who argue that this country was founded on secular, Enlightenment theories, and that the Founding Fathers and Framers desired to factor God out of the civil equation. But as has already been demonstrated, in view of the evidence, such an idea is absolutely untenable. For example, James Madison believed:

> *It is the duty of every man to render to the Creator such homage and such only as he believes to be acceptable to him. This duty is precedent, both in order of time and in degree of obligation, to the claims of Civil Society.... And if a member of Civil Society, who enters into any subordinate Association, must always do it with a reservation of his duty to General Authority; much more must every man who becomes a member of any particular Civil Society, do it with a saving of his allegiance to the Universal Sovereign.*[3]

This concise and most articulate statement from the author of the First Amendment to the U. S. Constitution belies the claim that the Founding Fathers and Framers of the Constitution desired to factor God out of the civil equation. Nevertheless, the secular critics are quite implacable, insisting that "life, liberty, and the pursuit of happiness" are Enlightenment, not biblical, ideas. Well, let's examine these concepts and see if there is any truth to this claim.

---

[3] James Madison *et al.*, "Memorial and Remonstrance against Religious Assessments," June 20, 1785.

The Origin Of "Life"

As our Creator,[4] God is the source of all life, "for in Him we live and move and have our being."[5] Thus man, the creature, who is wonderfully made in the image of his Creator, has an inherent and inalienable "right to life"—a right which can be justifiably defended against all interlopers. But without God, the Creator and Lawgiver—the God who the secularists diligently and methodically work to diminish in the minds of the public—the State becomes the highest moral authority. When this happens, and it's happening right now in our society, rights, whether they be to life, liberty, or the pursuit of happiness, are no longer thought to be inalienable,[6] but are instead subject to the give and take of man-made think-sos. As a result, the inherent, God-given "right to life" has been seriously eroded in our culture, as the triune maladies of abortion, infanticide and euthanasia tragically attest.

Thankfully, the Founding Fathers knew better than to establish government on the whims of sentiment. Instead, they grounded the government they were founding on the bedrock of eternal truths, truths they believed to be "self-evident." This, more than anything else, demonstrates that these men were appealing to a biblically based way of knowing or epistemology, as the philosophers are fond of calling it. Such truths, the apostle Paul tells us, some men will be disposed to suppress "in unrighteousness."[7] This was not just something that was going to be limited to Paul's time, but would be the pattern that would manifest itself over and over

---

4   See Genesis 1 and 2.
5   Acts 17:28a.
6   Whether spelled "unalienable," as the Framers spelled it, or inalienable, the words have exactly the same meaning.
7   Romans 1:18.

again. That those of this kind are at work in our culture is something we are constantly reminded of almost everywhere we look and in practically everything we hear.

Paul further informs us that these truth suppressors are without excuse, for such truths are "manifest in them,"[8] which is just another way of saying "self-evident." I suggest a reading of Romans 1 and 2 with this in view and I think we'll all be able to agree with Paul and the Founding Fathers that such individuals are without any excuse for trying to deny these self-evident truths. Make no mistake about it, when these self-evident truths are effectively suppressed in the minds of a people, God gives them over to a "debased mind."[9] In such a condition, they

> *do those things which are not fitting; being filled with all unrighteousness, sexual immorality, wickedness, covetousness, maliciousness; full of envy, murder, strife, deceit, evil-mindedness; they are whisperers, backbiters, haters of God, violent, proud, boasters, inventors of evil things, disobedient to parents, undiscerning, untrustworthy, unloving, unforgiving, unmerciful; who knowing the righteous judgment of God, that those who practice such things are worthy of death, not only do the same but also approve of those who practice them.*[10]

Clearly, such an array of sins does not bode well for any nation, but such are, I am sad to say, indicative of the sin-laden avenue this country is traveling down. I say "down," for any nation that forgets God eventually goes down to the pit, according to Psalm 9:17. That this is a 180 degree turn from the self-evident

---

8 Romans 1:19.
9 Romans 1:28.
10 Romans 1:28b-32.

truths upon which the Founding Fathers grounded this nation is clear from an honest examination of history. Now, I am certainly not speaking here of the revisionist clap-trap that so often passes for history today. Instead, I mean history fairly reported.

As mentioned earlier, Benjamin Hart, in his book *Faith & Freedom*, said:

> *Even if one does not accept the truth of the Christian faith, prudence argues for the promulgation of its moral code in every area of public life, because history has demonstrated that Christian morality is indispensable to the preservation of a free society.*[11]

Thus, as America now seems intent on cutting itself off from its founding principles, it is safe to say that the "right to life," when considered at all, will continue to undergo the radical modification the secularists have envisioned. However, it is clear that such thinking was not evident among our Founding Fathers. The right to life they spoke of in the Declaration was a gift from God.

The Origin Of "Liberty"

Although the Bible speaks directly of "liberty" in the Old and New Testaments, it is referring primarily to the spiritual liberty that comes in connection with Jesus Christ, not the physical freedom we are usually referring to when we use this word. However, this is not to concede that there is an absence of this latter idea in the Scriptures, for if man is not free to exercise himself as a servant of God, which is, after all, "the whole duty of man,"[12] then he

---

[11] Hart, page 15.
[12] Ecclesiastes 12:13-14.

cannot be held responsible for his lack of service. In other words, if man isn't a free moral agent, then he can't be amenable to God's law. Consequently, Genesis 1 is the place to go in order to see the origin and importance of liberty/freedom.

God created man in His own image. In doing so, He endowed him with certain faculties and invested him with the authority to subdue the earth and have dominion over its creatures.[13] Therefore, from the creation mandate itself it can be necessarily inferred that man must have the liberty (i.e., the freedom) to obediently exercise himself in the performance of his God-given duties. Man, then, because he is man, ought to be free, and such liberty is not derived from other men, but from God Himself. Thus, liberty is intrinsic and, as such, is a "self-evident" "unalienable" "right," just as our Founding Fathers believed and said. Liberty, freedom, and being free were not just Enlightenment concepts, as the secularists claim, but ideas built right into the very fabric of things from the very beginning.

Unfortunately, the secular propagandists are firmly entrenched today. As such, they have convinced many, perhaps even most, to think that liberty is something derived from the State and, thus, a privilege. But quite to the contrary, liberty derives from God and is, therefore, a right that will be protected by God-ordained government. Any government that does not think this so is in league with the Devil (i.e., it is a Revelation 13 government), and will be a bane upon, not a blessing to, its citizens.

Thus, liberty is an essential right of man, just as God's word teaches and our Founding Fathers believed.

---

[13] See Genesis 1:26-28.

The Origin Of "The Pursuit Of Happiness"

Of the three rights mentioned in the Declaration of Independence, this one, many think, is proof positive that it was a creation of Enlightenment thought,[14] void of God and teeming with humanistic ideas. The "pursuit of happiness" idea seems to be more hedonistic than biblical, but this is not the way it is at all. Jefferson appears to have taken the phrase from the Virginia Constitution of 1776, which mentioned "pursuing and obtaining happiness and safety." The term "happiness" had a technical meaning in the English common law and would have conveyed a particular idea to the Founding Fathers. This is mirrored in Sir William Blackstone's *Commentaries on the Laws of England* (1765), where he said that God, the Creator, had "so inseparably interwoven the laws of eternal justice with the happiness of each individual, that the latter cannot be attained but by observing the former, and if the former be punctually obeyed, it cannot but induce the latter."

Thus, the "pursuit of happiness," as we begin to see, is not something inherently hedonistic at all. It was, instead, an idea well established among the people of that time, an idea that dealt with the self-evident truth that man's inalienable right to pursue happiness in the course of, and by attending to, his God-given obligations and responsibilities was something that could not be interfered with by the State. On the contrary, the State was to protect such a right with force, if necessary.[15] I like what Gary T. Amos said about this:

---

14 Henry Steele Commanger, *Jefferson, Nationalism, and the Enlightenment*, 1976, page 88.
15 See Romans 13:1-7.

> *Like other Christian concepts that became part of formal philosophy and the common law, the Biblical notion of happiness runs deep within the channels of the common law. Its use is so obvious and extensive in the growth of English legal thought, one wonders whether those today who call it an Enlightenment term have read anything at all from the source materials of the common law, materials that were well-known and widely read by the American founders.*[16]

Thus, we can see that the Founding Fathers, appealing as they did in the first paragraph of the Declaration to "The Laws of Nature and Nature's God" (i.e., the *natural revelation* that comes from the created order and the *special revelation* found in the Bible), created a government that was grounded in religious concepts best described as totally Christian. I say this because none of the delegates assembled from the thirteen states on that July 4, 1776 signing of the Declaration were Muslims, Buddhists, Confucianists, or Hindus, and almost half had some form of seminary training or degree. Yes, it is true that Jefferson had Deist leanings, but all the others would have certainly considered themselves to be Christians. But even the Deists of that day, particularly Jefferson, were fervent believers in the Judeo-Christian God who had revealed Himself both in nature and the Bible—hence the reference to "The Laws of Nature and Nature's God" in the Declaration of Independence. Suffice it to say that Jefferson, who was the principle architect of the document, wasn't a thirty-second cousin to modern secular, anti-God, humanists. I like what Richard John Neuhaus had to say about this:

---

[16] Amos, page 121.

The founding creed—"We hold these truths to be self-evi-dent"—affirms truths that have been and are today far from self-evident to the great majority of humankind. The truth that "all men are created equal, that they are endowed by their Creator with certain unalienable rights, that among these are life, liberty, and the pursuit of happiness" is a truth that can only be explained as the product of a very particular history. In the eighteenth century, its explication and popular acceptance can only be explained in the context of the taken-for-granted reality of Christian America. This is not to say that the truths affirmed by the Declaration cannot be supported by rigorously secular arguments that are not dependent upon the biblical tradition.... But, in view of the many attempts that have failed, skepticism about that possibility is in order. And there is the inherent difficulty of what to do with the Creator—a reference that in the logic of the Declaration is essential to the claim that human rights are prior to government in the order of both time and authority.[17]

Thus, the words and ideas articulated in the Declaration were biblical, not secular, and came not as a result of the humanism of the Enlightenment, as the secularists falsely claim, but from a long line of thinking that could only be described as "Judeo-Christian."

This is why that in the final paragraph of the Declaration, after a long list of grievances, appeal was made to "the Supreme Judge of the world" coupled with "a firm reliance on the protection of Divine Providence." So although it can be rightly argued that Jefferson exhibited a decidedly anti-religious, anti-clergy bent,

---

[17] *First Things*, "The End Of Abortion And The Meanings Of 'Christian America,'" June/July 2001.

he was definitely not anti-God. This is further illustrated by a rhetorical question Jefferson asked on another occasion in 1782:

And can the liberties of a nation be thought secure when we have removed their only firm basis, a conviction in the minds of the people that their liberties are the gift of God?[18]

But in defense of Jefferson's anti-religious, anti-clergy leanings (but not his Deism, of course), it is safe to say that many of us New Testament Christians would have had a very difficult time in colonial America, which was pretty much dominated by the three major denominations: the Congregationalists, the Presbyterians, and the Episcopalians. In fact, data indicate that on the eve of the Revolution perhaps no more than twenty percent of the American people were what we'd call "churched."[19] Keep in mind that the emerging groups, like the Baptists, Methodists, *et cetera*, didn't count in such tallying. Remember, also, that it was just such an environment that would eventually give birth to what is commonly referred to as the Restoration Movement. So, we New Testament Christians would no doubt have also had our troubles, as did Jefferson, with the established religion of that day. But to argue, as some do, that these folks did not believe in the God of the Bible is to totally misread the religious history and sentiment of that day, for they were, by and large, a God-fearing, religious people. With this established, it brings us back to the difference between a *right* and a *privilege*.

Believing that England had violated the laws of nature and of nature's God, *appealing* to the one Supreme Judge in the affairs of

---

[18] Notes On The State Of Virginia, Query XVIII, in Paul L. Ford, ed., *The Writing of Thomas Jefferson*, Volume III, 1894, page 267.
[19] Robert Finke and Rodney Starke, *The Churching of America, 1776-1990: Winners and Losers in Our Religious Economy*, 1992, pages 15-16.

men and nations, and *trusting* in the protection of Divine Providence, the Founding Fathers were *determined* to establish a government that would carefully, but vigorously, defend the God-given rights of its citizens. This, they believed, was the mandate of God-ordained government. They wrote of "unalienable" rights because they believed such to be sacrosanct, that is to say, inviolable. Such rights the State could never breach, they believed, but must always protect. It was precisely this kind of State that the Founding Fathers intended to create on July 4, 1776.[20]

It was not a democracy, as it was to be falsely dubbed by some, but a democratic republic: a unique order of government *of*, *by*, and *for* the people. Unique, because it was something much different than the monarchies that were in play up to that time. As Larry Schweikart and Michael Allen aptly put it in *A Patriot's History of the United States*:

> *...The story of how they invented America is crucial in understanding the government that has served the United States for more than two hundred years, and, more broadly, the growth of republican institutions in Western civilization. John Adams knew the opportunities and perils posed by separation from England and the formation of a new government, noting that he and his contemporaries had been "thrown into existence at a period when the greatest philosophers and lawgivers of antiquity would have wished to live. A period when a coincidence of circumstances...has afforded*

---

[20] If you have not yet done so, now would be a good time to read the entire Declaration, which is reproduced in Appendix A.

to the thirteen Colonies...an opportunity of beginning government anew from the foundation.[21]

They went on to say in that same paragraph:

Contrary to popular belief, the American Federal Constitution was not an immediate and inevitable result of the spirit of 1776. Indeed, briefly in March 1783, some questions existed about whether an army mutiny over pay might not result either in a military coup or Washington relenting to pressures to "take the crown," as one colonel urged him to do. Instead, Washington met with the ringleaders, and while putting on his eyeglasses, shattered their hostility by explaining that he had "not only grown gray but almost blind in service to my country."[22] Their resistance melted, as did the neonatal movement to make him king—though the regal bearing stayed draped over him until the end. As late as 1790, Franklin observed of Washington's walking stick, "If it were a scepter, he would have merited it."[23] More than anyone, Washington knew that he had helped found a republic and for that reason, if no other, his presence at the Constitutional Convention was important, if not necessary.[24]

So, what is the nature of republican government? is the question to be answered. We have grown accustomed to hearing that we are a democracy, but this was never the intent of the Founding Fathers. Instead, they established a republic, not a democracy, and

---

[21] 2004, page 88. Their citation for this is Winthrop Jordan and Leon Litwack, *The United States*, combined ed., 7th ed., 1991, page 131.
[22] *Ibid.*, pages 88-89. Their citation is Joseph J. Ellis, *Founding Brothers: The Revolutionary Generation*, 2002, page 130.
[23] *Ibid.*, Ellis, page 121.
[24] *Op. cit.*, pages 88-89.

this is illustrated by the anecdote where, having concluded his work on the Constitution, Benjamin Franklin walked outside and seated himself on a public bench. A woman approached him and asked, "Well, Dr. Franklin, what have you done for us?" To which Franklin is reported to have quickly responded, "My dear lady, we have given you a republic—if you can keep it." So, what then is the difference between a democracy and a republic?

A pure democracy operates by direct majority vote of the people. When an issue is to be decided, the entire population votes on it; the majority wins—thus the expression, "majority rule." Although this is what many are ignorantly clamoring for today, such would be a sheer disaster. James Madison, who is considered to be the "Father of the Constitution," because he was the principal author of the document, said this about democracies: "[D]emocracies have ever been spectacles of turbulence and contention; have ever been found incompatible with personal security, or the rights of property; and have, in general, been as short in their lives as they have been violent in their deaths."[25] Fisher Ames, who along with Madison, wrote the language of the First Amendment, said this: "A democracy is a volcano which conceals the fiery materials of its own destruction. These will produce an eruption and carry desolation in their way."[26] Seven years later he said, "The known propensity of a democracy is to licentiousness which the ambitious call, and ignorant believe to be, liberty."[27] I could go on and on with quotes from the Founding Fathers, but suffice it to say that they considered a democracy (or "mobocracy," as they liked to call it),

---

[25] Alexander Hamilton, John Jay, James Madison, *The Federalist on the New Constitution*, 1818, page 53, #10.

[26] Fisher Ames, "Speech on Biennial Elections," January 1788, in *Works of Fisher Ames*, 1809, page 24.

[27] *Ibid.*, "The Dangers of American Liberty," February 1805, page 384.

to be a plague to good government and therefore something to be avoided at all cost.

In contrast to a pure democracy, which is rule according to the will of the majority of the people at a specific time in history, which could well be described as "whims of the people," lacking any legal safeguard of the rights of the individual and the minority, a democratic republic is a government ruled by law with the assistance of duly elected representatives of the people. It could be further described as a government where the majority is limited by a written Constitution that seeks to safeguard the rights of the individual and the minority. But as we've seen from this study, the question remains: From whence do the laws governing such a form of government derive?

According to the great lexicographer Noah Webster, who as a young man served as a Connecticut Militiaman in the American Revolution, "[O]ur citizens should early understand that the genuine source of correct republican principles is the Bible, particularly the New Testament, or the Christian religion."[28] As a result, then, of the transcendent values derived from the "Law of Nature and Nature's God," that which I'm calling the Law above the law principle, the inalienable "right to Life" is absolutely unassailable by anyone, especially the State.

But unfortunately, this has now all changed. America's loss of faith in those principles the Founding Fathers worked so hard to give us has produced a government that no longer sees the right to Life as an absolute, unassailable right. Instead, the almighty State, that is to say, the idolized State, the one bowed down to as if it were a god, has become the grantor of not just *certain* privileges, but *all* of them. As such, it no longer grants the "privilege of Life"

---

[28] Noah Webster, *History of the United States*, 1832, page 6.

to unborn human beings in their mothers' wombs. Instead, the blood of many millions of unborn babies lies exposed on the otherwise barren rock of this nation's shame, crying out in righteous indignation for the wrath of God's judgment on a nation that permits such an ungodly thing to be done in its midst.

The Modern Idolized State Has Become The Grantor Of Privileges Rather Than The Protector Of Rights

Therefore, we have learned the hard way (i.e., by experience) that the State's view of "a right" versus "a privilege" has serious consequences. For example, can anyone think the Founding Fathers would not roll over in their graves, providing they could, at the thought of a mother being granted the State's permission to kill her unborn child? In fact, if the seven Supreme Court Justices who in 1973 voted to overturn all state and federal laws outlawing or restricting abortion that were inconsistent with their views would have held to the principles stated in the Declaration and later in the Constitution, they could have never ruled as they did, granting permission for abortion for any reason a woman chooses, up until the "point at which the fetus becomes 'viable,' that is, potentially able to live outside the mother's uterus. Viability is usually placed at about seven months (28 weeks) but may occur earlier, even at 24 weeks."[29] The Court also held that abortion, even after viability, must be available when needed to protect a woman's health, which the Court defined broadly in a companion case, basically granting permission to abort the unborn child anytime after conception and before birth.

---

[29] *Roe v. Wade*, 410 U.S., 113, January 22, 1973.

Law By Judicial Fiat

Ever since that black day in January 1973, those who favor abortion have screamed from the housetops about their "Constitutional right" to abortion. But, in truth, there is no constitutional right for any such thing. In *Roe v. Wade* and its companion case, *Doe v. Bolten*, the Supreme Court, instead of interpreting the Constitution, was actually engaged in judicial activism, creating law by judicial fiat rather than allowing it to be done through the legislative process. This has been affirmed by those on both sides of the issue. John Hart Ely, a Yale professor and, himself, a proponent of abortion, has described the Court's decision as "frightening." According to him: "The problem with Roe is not so much that it bungles the question it sets for itself, but rather that it sets a question the Constitution has not made the Court's business.... It is bad because it is bad constitutional law, or rather because it is not constitutional law and gives almost no sense of an obligation to try to be."[30] Professor John T. Noonan, Jr., who was then professor of law at the University of California (Berkeley), said: "...none of the existing legislation on abortion conformed to the Court's criteria. By this basic fact alone [the decision] may stand as the most radical decision ever issued by the Supreme Court."[31] Archibald Cox, of Watergate-prosecution fame, said what should be obvious to all fair-minded men and women: "The decisions plainly... sweep away established law supported by the moral themes dominant in American life for more than a century in favor of what the Court takes to be a wiser view of a question under active debate.... My criticism of [the decision] is that the Court failed to establish the legitimacy

---

[30] *Yale Law Journal*, 82: 943,947.
[31] *Human Life Review*, 1:28, 1975.

of the decision...[and] to lift the ruling above the level of political judgment."[32]

Professor Felix Frankfurter, who himself became a Supreme Court Justice, wrote to Franklin Roosevelt in 1937: "People have been taught to believe that when the Supreme Court speaks it is not they who speak but the Constitution, whereas, of course, in so many vital cases, it is they who speak and not the Constitution. And I verily believe that is what the country needs most to understand."[33] Consequently, it is hard for many people to believe that the highest court in the land is steeped in political activism, exalting their own think-sos above the Constitution, but this is exactly the case.

That this is unquestionably true was pointed out by Justice W. O. Douglas who recounted that when he came to the Court, Chief Justice Hughes "made a statement to me which at the time was shattering but which over the years turned out to be true: 'Justice Douglas, you must remember one thing. At the constitutional level...ninety percent of any decision is emotional. The rational part of us supplies the reasons for supporting our predilections'... I knew that judges had predilections.... But I had never been willing to admit to myself that the 'gut' reaction of a judge at the level of constitutional adjudications dealing with the vagaries of due process...was the main ingredient of his decision. The admission of it destroyed in my mind some of the reverence for immutable principles."[34] Add to this the words of former Chief Justice Frederick Moore Vinson, who said, "Nothing is more certain in modern society than the principle that there are no absolutes," and the evidence is conclusive that the Supreme Court, instead of interpreting

---

[32] *The Role of the Supreme Court in America*, 1976.
[33] *Roosevelt and Frankfurter: Their Correspondence, 1928-1945*, page 383.
[34] *Zorach v. Clauson*, 343, U.S. 306, 314.

the Constitution, and in direct contradiction of the desires of the Founding Fathers, has actually been engaged in its own ongoing "Constitutional Convention."

It is interesting just here to notice what, some two hundred years earlier, the Anti-federalist writer known as "Brutus," who was probably New York's Judge Robert Yates, had to say about the famous "checks and balances" the Federalists, particularly Madison, were claiming would be sufficient to keep the federal judiciary from getting out of hand. In a series of essays published in the *New York Journal*, which became known as the Anti-federalist Papers, Judge Yates, who had been a delegate to the Constitutional Convention and withdrew because he believed it was exceeding its instructions, in an especially prescient manner, wrote:

> *The real effect of this system of government, will therefore be brought home to the feelings of the people, through the medium of the judicial power. It is, moreover, of great importance, to examine with care the nature and extent of the judicial power, because those who are to be vested with it, are to be placed in a situation altogether unprecedented in a free country. They are to be rendered totally independent, both of the people and the legislature, both with respect to their offices and salaries. No errors they may commit can be corrected by any power above them, if any such power there be, nor can they be removed from office for making ever so many erroneous adjudications.*
>
> *The only causes for which they can be displaced, is, conviction of treason, bribery, and high crimes and misdemeanors.*
>
> *This part of the plan is so modeled, as to authorize the courts, not only to carry into execution the powers expressly*

*given, but where these are wanting or ambiguously expressed,
to supply what is wanting by their own decisions.*[35]

Writing specifically of the Supreme Court, he went on to say:

*They will give the sense of every article of the constitution,
that may from time to time come before them. And in their
decisions they will not confine themselves to any fixed or established rules, but will determine, according to what appears to them, the reason and spirit of the constitution. The
opinions of the supreme court, whatever they may be, will
have the force of law; because there is no power provided in
the constitution, that can correct their errors, or control their
adjudications. From this court there is no appeal.*[36]

He went on to predict that freed from the constraints imposed
by the Constitution, there would be no practicable limits to the
Court's all-encompassing reach:

*When the courts will have a precedent before them of a court
which extended its jurisdiction in opposition to an act of the
legislature, is it not to be expected that they will extend theirs,
especially when there is nothing in the constitution expressly
against it, and they are authorised to construe its meaning,
and are not under any control?*

*This power in the judicial, will enable them to mold the
government, into almost any shape they please.*[37]

Finally:

---

[35] Robert Yates, "Essay No. 11," *Anti-federalist Papers*, first published in
the *New York Journal*, March 20, 1788.
[36] *Ibid.*
[37] *Ibid.*

*Perhaps nothing could have been better conceived to facilitate
the abolition of the state governments than the constitution
of the judicial. They will be able to extend the limits of the
general government gradually, and by insensible degrees,
and to accommodate themselves to the temper of the people.
Their decisions on the meaning of the constitution will commonly take place in cases which arise between individuals,
with which the public will not be generally acquainted; one
adjudication will form a precedent to the next, and this to a
following one.*[38]

In summary, and in the words of Richard Neuhaus, Yates pre-
dicted that far from the courts being checked by the legislative and
executive branches, these two latter branches would eventually
"acquiesce and even collude in the protection and expansion of
government power by letting the judiciary have the last word in
saying what the Constitution means."[39] He also said the Supreme
Court would adopt "very liberal" principles of interpreting the
Constitution and, of course, this is exactly what happened. As a result, "rights" today are no longer considered to be antecedent (i.e.,
God-given), as our Founding Fathers believed, but are instead simply concocted by the Court whenever and however it pleases. As a
result, that which Alexander Hamilton, in Federalist 78, thought
would be "the least dangerous branch" of government has become,
in point of fact, the one with terribly "immense power," just as the
prescient Yates had feared.

Thus, the ongoing Constitutional Convention mentality, em-
powered as it is by a humanistic, arbitrary, and sociological outlook concerning the law, has brought us to our current

---

[38] "Brutus 15," *Anti-federalist Papers*, available at www.constitution.org.
[39] See "We Are the State" in *First Things*, December 28, 2007.

Constitutional crises, which asks: *How is it possible for written or abstract law (viz., the U.S. Constitution), which is based upon certain moral absolutes (i.e., the inalienable rights endowed by our Creator), to be interpreted fairly by those who actually believe there is no adequate base for law except human sentiment?* This crises has been playing out all around us for some time now. A prominent case in point is the 1987 Congressional rejection of former President Reagan's nomination of Robert Bork to the Supreme Court. Judge Bork was an "originalist" who had been quite vocal in his rejection of the judicial activism that produced the *Roe v. Wade* decision. According to Mark R. Levin, one of America's preeminent conservative commentators and constitutional lawyers, and a good friend of Bork, "Originalists believe that the powers enumerated specifically in the Constitution are the only powers of the federal government, unless the Constitution is formally amended."[40] Such are also identified as "strict constructionists," and are, unfortunately, a dying breed. Commenting on this, the syndicated columnist James Kilpatrick said:

> *We pride ourselves on saying that ours is a government of law, not men, but the boast is empty. It is a myth, a shibboleth, a sham. At the level of the Supreme Court, ours is emphatically not a government of abstract law but a government of eight very mortal men and one woman.*[41]

Those who were instrumental in the rejection of Judge Bork knew that this is true and, consequently, they did not want him, as a strict constructionist, to be in a position to overturn *Roe v. Wade.*

---

40 Mark R. Levin, *Men In Black: How the Supreme Court Is Destroying America*, 2005, page 13.
41 *Courier-Journal*, Louisville, KY, July 15, 1982, page A15.

As a result, not only did they successfully "Bork" him, but they have "Borked" any potential judge whom they think to be an originalist ever since. Now, with Bork's defeat, Ronald Reagan first nominated Judge Douglas Ginsburg, who decided to step down when his previous pot-smoking was made public. He then nominated Judge Anthony Kennedy, who was supposed to be a judicial conservative, but wasn't. Justice Kennedy, who could have voted to overturn *Roe v. Wade* in the 1992 case of *Planned Parenthood v. Casey* (and there's no doubt that Bork would have), made a last-moment switch, according to Justice Harry Blackmun's personal papers, siding with the four other justices who wished to preserve *Roe*. As he continued to "evolve," Kennedy turned out, along with O'Connor, to be one of two so-called "swing votes." Therefore, we can see that the defeat of Judge Robert H. Bork's nomination to the Supreme Court was not just a tragedy for Judge Bork, but it was a critical turning point in the righteous effort to reverse the moral malignancy that has ravaged millions upon millions of unborn Americans in their mothers' wombs since that fateful November day some thirty-five years ago.

Since then, anyone nominated to the Supreme Court who the liberals think might be likely to reverse *Roe*, if given the chance, has been labeled "out of the mainstream" of current American jurisprudence. We have heard the charge made over and over again, and it has been very effective. In fact, the whole nominating process has been changed dramatically. With Senators now acting as the protectors of what they have erroneously determined, for social and political reasons, to be the orthodox judicial doctrine, Supreme Court nominees have been forced to actively politic for their appointments, essentially making campaign promises not to upset the liberal judicial apple cart. This, in effect, is what now Chief Justice Roberts did, and this is why I was so disappointed with George W. Bush and the political game he had consented to play.

In his insightful book, *The Tempting Of America: The Political Seduction Of The Law*, published in 1990, Judge Bork had this to say about his defeat:

> *The greatest impact of what occurred, however, may not be simply the precedent set but what the knowledge that such a campaign is always possible will do to the calculations of other actors in the process.*[42]

He went on to say:

> *A president who wants to avoid a battle like mine, and most presidents would prefer to [do so], is likely to nominate men and women who have not written much, and certainly nothing that could be regarded as controversial by left-leaning senators and groups. People who have thought much about the role proper to judges are likely, however, to have written or spoken on the subject. The tendency, therefore, will be to nominate and confirm persons whose performance once on the bench cannot be accurately, or perhaps even roughly, predicted either by the President or by the Senate.*[43]

Finally, he said in the same place:

> *When the Court is perceived as a political rather than a legal institution, nominees will be treated like political candidates, campaigns will be waged in public, lobbying of senators and the media will be intense, the nominee will be questioned about how he will vote, and he will be pressed to*

---

42 Page 346.
43 Page 348.

make campaign promises about adhering to or rejecting particular doctrines.

What Judge Bork feared is now a reality we have all seen played out before our own eyes in the nomination and appointment of Chief Justice John G. Roberts, Jr. *et al.* Roberts was even assigned an actor *cum* politician *cum* television star to "shmooze" senators and other key players in this highly politicized game. He made his campaign promises, making it clear that he believes that: "*Roe Vs. Wade* is the settled law of the land.... There's nothing in my personal views that would prevent me from fully and faithfully applying that precedent." Consequently, Roberts was all but confirmed when nominated by the President. There would be only token resistance from the usual suspects. Then, when Bush got another opportunity, he nominated Ms. Harriet Miers, who Robert Bork, speaking from his originalist point of view, called a "disaster." When she withdrew after opposition from conservative sources continued to mount, Bush nominated Samuel A. Alito, Jr., who was eventually confirmed by the Senate after signaling (you might think of it as a campaign promise) that he would be highly reluctant to overturn long-standing precedents such as the 1973 *Roe v. Wade* decision, which was, in essence, the same promise Roberts had made.

Obviously, George W. Bush was a grave disappointment to originalists by capitulating to power politics, surrendering his integrity to what now seems like a shameful lie that promised the appointment of originalists as judges[44]—a lie that served to provide

---

[44] A judge who claims to be an originalist, but bows to the principle of *stare decises*, as both Roberts and Alito promised to do, are clearly lacking originalist *bona fides.*

him the margin of victory he needed in both of his elections, which is, as I see it, a shameful, sordid, and disgraceful thing!

Sadly, the *Roe v. Wade* decision was only the implementation of an idea long expressed by those prominent in the law profession; namely, "When it comes to the development of a [body of law] the ultimate question is what do the dominant forces of the community want and do they want it hard enough to disregard whatever inhibitions may stand in the way."[45] How badly did the humanists want the selfish, degrading, and utterly inhumane "right" to abortion? Badly enough to have made it their number one priority in the late sixties and early seventies of the twentieth century.

But as terrible as abortion is, it was only the opening of "Pandora's Box." When it was decided that babies in their mothers' wombs do not have the right-to-life, the demons of infanticide and euthanasia were also let loose. These are but a few of the moral dilemmas facing modern man. Test-tube babies, embryo transplants, genetic manipulation, eugenics, cryobiology, *et cetera*, are more examples of the plethora of technologies that are inundating and sweeping away forever the ethical and moral principles that have made us who we are. Many of the hard, tough decisions we talked about in the early eighties of the last century have now been made and we are reading about them in our newspapers and seeing and hearing about them on our televisions. Unfortunately, too many of these decisions are being made incorrectly. The Biblically rooted ethical base that had served us so well in the past must be resurrected or our culture, as we have come to know it, will

---

[45] Found in a letter from Oliver Wendell Holmes, Jr. to John C.H. Wu, August 26, 1926, published in Harry C. Shriver, ed., *Justice Oliver Wendell Holmes: His Book Notices and Uncollected Letters and Papers*, page 187.

forever cease to be. The lid to Pandora's Box cannot be easily put back in its place. And even if we are able to do so, I am afraid the phantoms that have already been released will continue to haunt us and seduce us in the coming years.

Ideas Have Consequences

Ideas do, in fact, have consequences.[46] Our Founding Fathers knew this and hitched this nation's star to the "self-evident" and "unalienable" rights granted by the one and only Sovereign of the universe. Secular humanists know this and are doing their best to unhitch us from the Sovereign of the universe and replace Him with the ever-changing think-sos of human sentiment.

How, then, does all this apply to the issue at hand? Simply this: Somewhere along the way, and I'm not sure just exactly where, America's Democratic Republic, a truly magnificent creation, started to lean toward becoming an imperialist State. In some areas it has begun to exhibit decidedly Revelation 13 machinations. Judge Bork, in a 1996 book, identified this trend as "Slouching toward Gomorrah."[47] Consequently, the citizen's God-given rights to Life, Liberty, and the Pursuit of Happiness have been co-opted by a State that too often does not see itself as the protector of these rights but, instead, the grudging grantor. Under such a State, God-given rights are abrogated and His law circumvented.

Little "g" gods, just like the big "G" God, don't like competition. Thus, the idolized State will seek, where it can, to denude the

---

[46] This concept is stated in Proverbs 23:7, which says, "For as he thinketh in his heart, so is he" (KJV).

[47] Roberk H. Bork, *Slouching Toward Gomorrah: Modern Liberalism and American Decline*, 1996.

influence of the one and only true God. It does not want its citizens to be subject to any authority higher than itself, thus it attempts to remove every vestige of the *I Am That I Am* from society. This has been done rather slowly and sometimes imperceptively up to now, but as new ways of thinking, and the new ideas that come from such thinking, take hold, the process will begin to pick up speed until God is totally expunged. Assisting in this effort is a new Concilium,[48] for as secular humanism has become the new religion of the State, secular humanists have become its priesthood, demanding obeisance (the burning of a little incense) to the State (i.e., to Caesar) as the giver of every good and perfect gift, and this *vis-à-vis* its ever present social and welfare programs. This new Concilium uses its historically incorrect view of

---

[48] When studying the history that is contemporary to the Roman Emperor Domitian, one comes across an organization that acted as the enforcer for Domitian's religious policies. This was the Concilia. It was a "religious group" set in place by Domitian to support, regulate, and enforce emperor worship and see that the emperor's edicts were carried out throughout Asia Minor, the very place the bulk of the Christian persecutions were the worst. To a Christian, worshipping the emperor was forbidden regardless of the circumstances or hazard to personal lives. Christians were boycotted in the market places for failure to bear the stamp of the emperor. Marriages, wills, and real estate transactions were all illegal without the stamp of Domitian. The Concilia was given the legal authority to make sure that anybody who refused to purchase a little incense and burn it to Caesar as god would not be granted any legal status for conducting business in the Empire. Thus, the Christians who refused to worship the emperor were prohibited from having the official stamp which, if they were unable to produce it, meant any transaction with them would be illegal. When the Concilia spoke, they spoke as priests in the name of State religion. It had the authority to incarcerate offenders and haul them before the Roman officials. The penalty for refusing to worship could be as stiff as execution. For a further study of this, see Ray Summers, *Worthy Is The Lamb*, 1951, pages 178-179 and Henry Swete, *Commentary On Revelation*, 1911 (reprinted in 1977), pages 168ff.

the separation of Church and State principle to teach that the secular (read public) life of a people and its institutions must be totally cleansed of Jehovah Elohim, that One who claims to be King of kings and Lord of lords. No siree! None of that kind of thinking is going to be allowed by the idolized State.

At A Crossroads

America, I believe, is at a crossroads. Will its people ever return to the principles upon which the Republic was originally founded? If they attempt to do so, they must know they will have a monumental fight on their hands. There has been too much secular "water under the bridge" for it to be otherwise. The secularists effectively control the media and the educational establishment, two extremely powerful propaganda tools. Furthermore, the State, unencumbered by the moral absolutes upon which this nation was originally founded, has gotten habituated to throwing its weight around. The old "give 'em an inch, they'll take a mile" adage is quite *à propos* when it comes to the State. Instead of viewing the public school system as an adjunct of the Home and, therefore, something to which it simply lends its support, the State now sees it as an entity belonging to the State and a useful tool for the near universal dissemination of its propaganda. As such, God, along with anything that could be construed as being Judeo-Christian, is being effectively excised from the public school curriculum. The textbooks that supposedly teach early American history actually do no such thing, as "Nature and Nature's God" are either diminished or completely ignored. If you don't believe me, check it out for yourselves. In doing so, you will be shocked by what you will *not* find. The "Hell no, Western Civ. has got to go" bunch of the 1960s have all grown up and now control the State's primary propaganda machine.

Before it is too late, let us be determined, no matter what the cost, to return to our roots. Let us be determined to exercise the rights our Creator granted us—rights that entitle us to remind the State it is duty-bound to protect. If enough of us are willing to not just *stand up*, but to *speak out* on these very fundamental things, then perhaps those who come after us will be blessed by our efforts, as we decidedly were by those who put everything on the line to give us a unique form of government built on the solid foundation of God's eternal and self-evident truths. Like them, and "with a firm reliance on the protection of Divine Providence," let us "mutually pledge to each other our Lives, our Fortunes, and our sacred Honor."

Chapter 3

The American Revolution: Unholy Rebellion Or Holy Disobedience?

ecause rebellion is so clearly condemned in the Scriptures, many Christians have believed the American Revolution was inherently sinful. I believe they are wrong, and in the pages that follow, I will give my reasons why. In doing so, I will continue to capitalize on one of the main themes of this book, and that is that it is sometimes necessary to resist authority. I have dubbed such resistance, "holy disobedience." But it is important to note that in doing so, I have also argued that holy disobedience is not really rebellion at all, for rebellion, by biblical standards, is the sinful refusal to obey lawful authority. Therefore, what some call rebellion is, in truth, obedience to God rather than man.[1]

There must be no doubt that the Bible clearly teaches that lawful authority, whether in the Home, the Church, or the State, can *never* be rightly resisted. In other words, such disobedience is always sinful. Thus, if the American Revolution is to be successfully defended, then it must be demonstrated that the Colonies were not in rebellion at all, but were, instead, exercising their God-given duty to resist unlawful authority. If in the process of doing so, they found it necessary to jettison *not* lawful authority, which would have been wrong, but a tyrant, which is always the obligation of

---

1   See Acts 4:18-19; 5:27-29.

honorable men, then sin cannot attach to such actions, unless such is accomplished by anarchy. As we shall see, anarchy was not the means used by the Colonists, nor was it ever the intended goal.

The Anti-War Default

But for those who believe war is always wrong, the American Revolution could never be right. If you are of that persuasion, I cannot hope to convince you of the rightness of the spirit of 1776, for it is a story of war. If there is, in fact, no such thing as a just war (I like to call this the anti-war default), then the American Revolution was not just wrong, but sinfully so. For those who think this way, my thesis is already unsustainable. All I can do, then, is suggest you consider the more extensive arguments I make about war in my little book on that subject.[2]

The Anti-Disobedience Default

In the same vein, for those who believe it is always wrong to disobey those in positions of authority, and I like to refer to this position as the anti-disobedience default, I had hoped the arguments presented in this book up to this point would have convinced you otherwise. If they haven't, then for you, too, the American Revolution must always be wrong.

On the other hand, if you have come to see that holy disobedience is not just an option, but sometimes a requirement, then I may be able to convince you that the cause of the Colonists was right and just. So, if you agree with me that war is not always inherently sinful, that the exercise of tyrannical power is always

---

2 Allan Turner, *The Christian & War*, 2006.

wrong, and that it is always right to resist such power, then I hope to be able to convince you that the American Revolution continues to stand as a shining example of what holy disobedience and just war are all about.

However, before anyone can hope to pass righteous judgment on the American Revolution, it will be necessary for one to "get up to speed" on the major differences that existed in England and the American Colonies prior to July 4, 1776. The history that follows is not exhaustive by any stretch of the imagination, for it would take reams and reams to even try to be, and even then would still be quite incomplete. What follows, then, is an attempt to demonstrate the root cause of the Colonies' resistance to King George III, while identifying the basic reasons they gave for resisting him.

Tories And Whigs, Whigs And Tories

It has been my experience that anyone struggling with what the Bible says about rebellion and "the spirit of 1776" has probably given some thought to what party he would have aligned himself with during the American Revolution. Tories were Colonists who remained loyal to the British Crown up to and during the Revolution. Thus, they were also called Loyalists, the King's Men, and Royalists. Their opponents, who supported the American Revolution, were called Whigs, Patriots, Rebels, and Congress Men. Thus, these two parties, the Tories and the Whigs, represent the sharp division that existed in the Colonies prior to and during the American Revolution. Taking the time to understand these two parties goes a long way in helping one to comprehend the root causes of the Revolution or Rebellion, for depending upon what party you were a member of, or sympathetic to, you thought of it as being either one or the other.

The Tories' View Of Things

Historians have estimated that about 33% of the white population may have been Loyalists (that is, about 500,000), but there are no exact numbers. They, of course, saw themselves as the "honourable"[3] ones who stood by the Crown and the British Empire, which they believed to be the rightful authority under whom they were obligated to be obedient. So, it is clear that if the Tories were right, the American Revolution was nothing less than sinful rebellion. It will be my task, then, to refute the Tory view.

But before doing so, let me say that I suspect that many of my brethren today, if alive then, would have been Tories. There was even a time when I thought that I, too, would have been a Tory. I no longer think so. I attribute this to two things: (1) my continued study of God's word and (2) a more thorough understanding of the history and writings that led to the American Revolution. Therefore, if anything, I would have been a Whig. I say, "if anything," because it is always the possibility that I could have been totally apolitical; but I rather doubt it. What's more, the pacifists among us who I've talked to would surely have taken a hands-off position on the whole "nasty" thing, while all the while quietly or silently rooting for one side or the other. I say this because although my pacifist brethren think the Christian ought to never be involved in war, they nevertheless usually have some definite ideas about who they think should win such wars, especially when their own skin or bailiwick is at stake. In other words, they believe it would have been wrong for them to fight against the Germans and Japanese during WW II, for example, but they're sure glad the

---

[3]   This is the softer English spelling of the sharper American "honorable," and is something a Tory would have been very careful to maintain.

Allies fire-bombed German cities and atomized much of Hiroshima and Nagasaki in order to hasten that war to its "rightful" conclusion. But I digress. Again, if you're interested in a further study of this, consider my little book on war, where I deal with this in much more detail.[4]

For the sake of argument, and for the purpose of simplifying a rather complex set of circumstances, I am using the Tory and Whig parties to explain the two very different perspectives of the Colonialists up to and during the Revolution. This is not to say there were not more nuanced ideas on either side, only that the basic differences between these two parties pretty well sums up the major differences that ripped through the political-social fabric of the Colonies at the time of the Revolution.

The Puritans

Factored into this equation must also be the influence of the Puritans. In fact, the story of religion in America is the story of Puritanism. At the time of the Revolution, about three-quarters of the North American Colonists were of Puritan extraction. Without a doubt, it was the dominant political, religious, and intellectual force throughout the 17th and 18th centuries.[5] Therefore, given all the good things we owe to the Puritan legacy, it is disappointing how little most Americans actually know about them. In fact, the term Puritan actually carries with it a negative connotation today. Notwithstanding, it was Puritans who actually gave us "our first written constitutions, regular elections, the secret ballot, the federalist principle, and separation of Church and State."[6]

---

4   *The Christian & War.*
5   Hart, page 83.
6   *Ibid.*

Furthermore, it was their work ethic and their emphasis on equality under the law that spawned the capitalist spirit that triumphed over the hereditary privilege that had so dominated England.

It is even argued today that Puritanism failed. After all, there is not one single Puritan left to be found anywhere on the planet. But those who think this way are very much mistaken, for the Puritan spirit remains omnipresent in much of America, even to this day. I'll say more about this a bit further along, but before doing so, it is important to understand that Puritanism was never a formal Christian sect or denomination. The term, like now, was more a term of derision, and it is believed to have been first used by Queen Elizabeth who branded those who refused to conform to the *"Liturgie, Ceremonies and Discipline of the Church"* with the "invidious" name of "Puritane."[7]

Puritans, it is discovered, simply thought of themselves as Christians. What they had in common was a belief "that the official church was not a true Christian church in the sense of resembling the church established by Jesus and his Apostles."[8] To them, the Church of England or Anglican Church, as it was also known, was an abomination, for they believed that any church under the authority of a monarch was not really much different than one under the rule of a pope, and it can be safely said that they relished neither the Church of England nor the Church of Rome.

Consequently, Puritans were keen to attack anything resembling "popish" ritual in the English Church, and there was plenty of it to attack. In response, Queen Elizabeth said such people were "over bold with God Almighty, making too many subtle scannings of His Blessed Will." They were viewed as not just

---

7   *Ibid.*
8   *Op. cit.,* page 84.

trouble-makers, but downright subversives, as well. Writing in the 1630s, Thomas Hobbes, who will be discussed in more detail in Chapter 7, was of course a staunch supporter of monarchy, and expressed the sentiments of the ruling elites when he said that such people were poor security risks.

So, it seems, Puritanism was always associated with rebellion, and rebellion, most thought, was always wrong. However, rebellion was something most Puritans were reluctant to engage in, as they, too, thought such to be a sin. But when the government, and please keep in mind that their's was a government where the separation of Church and State did not exist, pressed them, as it frequently did, to choose between their monarch's will and what they believed to be God's will, there was absolutely no doubt whom they intended to obey.

But Puritans were not rebellious by nature. In fact, they believed that even an unjust and corrupt government was better than no government at all—at least up to a point. Just where that point happened to be was a question that could only be answered by individual conscience, and this only after applying the principles taught in the Bible. Speaking of this, Benjamin Hart perceptively wrote:

> *The point at which the individual Protestant in England decided to separate from, or rebel against, the established church varied, and thus had a bearing on the type of Protestants with whom he associated. The Episcopalian rejected the pope, but accepted bishops; the Presbyterian said no to bishops in favor of presbyters; Congregationalists shunned all ecclesiastical jurisdiction outside of the particular parish; Anabaptists were similar to Congregationalists, but were more radical in their separatist views. Perhaps more than any Christian sect, Anabaptists rejected human pronouncements*

*and accepted as authoritative only the unadorned word of
God. The branch of Protestantism one associated with usually had a bearing on one's politics. Episcopalians identified
more readily with aristocracy and Toryism; Presbyterianism
with republican government; Congregationalism with democracy; while Anabaptist Separatists tended to be hostile to
all man-made constructions, and might be considered liber-
tarian (though certainly not libertine). It was these kinds of
people, mainly Congregationalist and Separatist Protestants,
who, prodded by the royal and church bureaucracy, decided
in the 1630s to leave Old England for New England. It was a
mass exodus. They emigrated, in fact, in such numbers that it
must have appeared as though all of England was leaving.
They included men of wealth, education, and position: lawyers, doctors, merchants, college professors, and some of the
most famous evangelists and theologians.[9]*

To make a long and complicated history short and succinct,
the politics of Old England were very much associated with one's
religious perspective. All this evolved into two basic parties that
were very much tied to one's religious perspective: Whig/Puritan
and Tory/Anglican. It was these two parties, then, with their roots
very much in Old England, that are in play in New England and
the rest of the Colonies before and during the Revolution.

So with a better understanding of the political and religious
history of the two parties that were extant at the time of the Revolution, I can comfortably say that I would not have been at all inclined toward Toryism, and this for religious reasons more than
anything else. I would no doubt have seen my Tory friends and

---

9 *Op. cit.*, pages 84-85.

neighbors as dupes of the very system I had come to the Colonies to get away from—a Church-State system that by its very nature was coercive of individual conscience. Thus, it is time to take a look at the Whig party.

The Whigs' View

With the rise to the throne of Charles I, the Puritan/non-Catholic/non-conformist cause in England seemed to be dead. Under Queen Elizabeth and then King James, there was hope that the English Church might abandon its Romanized hierarchical structure. But with the ascent to the throne of Charles I, all hope was lost. To protect the Church-State relationship that vested in the British monarch all-encompassing power, Charles directed Archbishop William Laud to purge England of all those who attacked the "stately grandeur of his royal church."[10] The result was a terrible reign of terror. For criticizing the church, one could be branded and put in prison for life. In fact, these were the usual penalties. In addition, one could have his or her ears cropped and/or nostrils slit. There were also heavy fines, long prison terms in rodent-infested dungeons, all of which depended on just how egregious the offense was perceived to be. Because the Puritan/non-Catholic/non-conformist preachers were usually the more eloquent speakers, all sermons were outlawed. Innovative preachers took to calling their sermons "lectures," but these, too, were also banned. It was such persecution that caused flight to the New World, and the rest, as they say, is history.

The Laud purge and persecution in England had helped to bring to Massachusetts Bay and other places along the eastern

---

10 *Op. cit.*, page 86.

shores of the American continent, a group of people who were looking for the freedom to exercise themselves religiously as their consciences dictated. It matters not that these pilgrims established their own State churches, for one was not forced to live within any particular of these jurisdictions, but was free to move and live where one wanted to.

So, it can be seen that Puritans and those of their ilk pressed upon our shores to establish commonwealths in accordance with the understanding they had of the precepts found in God's word. Because the truths taught in the Bible and democratic institutions are compatible, Puritans and Whigs would eventually and easily coalesce into a formidable alliance that would stand against the Crown and those aligned with it, like the Tories/Anglicans.

Factor into all this the writings of John Locke *et al.,* along with the pamphleteering that was so prevalent in Colonial America, and you have a very well-read citizenry that rejected Thomas Hobbes' divine right of kings philosophy in favor of the Lockean concept of a government that exercises itself with the consent of the governed. Although this was a revolutionary idea for the time, it was a concept that, surprisingly, had been taught in God's word all along. I say surprisingly, because what the Bible actually taught on this subject had been grossly distorted by several factors.

One of these was the Hobbesian/Machiavellian justification of the government's right to exercise absolute power.[11] The other was the misinterpretation of Romans 13:1-7, which believed that the actual ordaining of a specific, particular government is what these verses are really all about (as opposed to the idea that government in general, a government that would have certain qualities, is

---

[11] Once again I ask you to refer to chapter 7, where this subject is dealt with in much more detail.

what was under discussion). From these evolved the so-called "Divine Right of Kings" doctrine that prevailed in England, at least in the minds of the monarchs and those who supported them, like the Tories/Anglicans.

The Divine Right Of Kings

The Divine Right of Kings is a doctrine of political absolutism and is the general term used for the ideas surrounding the authority and legitimacy of a Monarch. It broadly holds that a monarch derives his right to rule from the will of God, and not from any temporal authority, including the will of his subjects. Directly chosen by God, a monarch is accountable only to Him, and answers only to God for his actions. As King James I of England said in the *Basilikon Doron*,[12] a manual on the duties of a King, which was written in the form of a private and confidential letter to his eldest son, Henry, Prince of Wales, "Just as no misconduct on the part of a father can free his children from obedience to the fifth commandment, so no misgovernment on the part of a King can release his subjects from their allegiance."[13] This, then, along with his *The True Law of Free Monarchies*, which was published in 1598, is the best articulation of The Divine Right of Kings extant, and shows the mistake King James I and the Stuart kings who followed him made when it came to the exercise of their delegated authority. In *The True Law*, James wrote, "A good King will frame his actions to be according to the law, yet he is not bound thereto but of his good will." He also caused to be printed his book entitled *Defense of the Right of Kings*, which was designed to counter those

---

12 It was printed in Edinburgh in 1599 and in London in 1603.
13 See C. V. Wedgwood, *The King's Peace*, 1956, page 63.

who questioned the King's alleged God-given right to exercise absolute power. It claimed that the King was the supreme authority on earth and therefore not subject to any so-called "inferior" powers. In making these claims, King James was trying to put to rest the thinking of Puritans, those pesky non-conformists who viewed the King as a servant of God on the people's behalf and therefore subject to them, as well as to God.

Clearly, the Whigs/Puritans were conscientious objectors to the Divine Right of Kings. They believed that Romans 13:1-7 was speaking of government in general, namely, a government consisting of qualities that would cause it to support the doing of Justice and Righteousness, a government that would serve the people. I believe the Whigs/Puritans were right, of course, and it was precisely this kind of thinking that motivated the colonists to finally cut ties with the English Crown.[14] Thus, what started in 1776 in America was the continuation of a struggle that had been going on for quite some time.

In an effort to make fairly short the long and complicated journey to 1776, I have neglected many important developments, like the rise of the mislabeled Holy Roman Empire, along with the development of the apostate Roman Catholic Church which, along with its popes, wholeheartedly endorsed the line of emperors beginning with the Emperors Constantine and Theodosius, later the Eastern Roman emperors, and finally the Western

---

[14] For those interested in a better uderstanding of this development, they must spend some time studying the events that led up to Magna Carta and the profound influence this compact had on the development of the legal system in England and America. Two excellent books on this are Louis Wright's *Magna Carta and the Tradition of Liberty* (1976) and A. E. Dick Howard's *The Road From Runnymede: Magna Carta and Constitutionalism in America* (1968). Wright's book is a condensed treatment of professor Howard's more detailed work.

Roman emperor, Charlemagne. To counter the unchecked authority of the emperor/king, the Catholic Church developed the theory of "Two Swords." This taught that the only authority that could depose a monarch was the pope. This was not just an idea that remained theory, but was a power popes effectively exercised on more than one occasion. But with the rise of Protestantism, kings were left with nothing to check their power and therefore, if inclined, could be despots. As a result, the people suffered and it was the realities of this suffering that caused some to begin to closely examine what God actually said about these things in His word. So, although I haven't gone into all of this in great detail, such will be very interesting to anyone wanting to study these things in depth.

Finally, the writings of King James were intended to be critical of papists and Puritans, for these, for very different reasons, were rightly viewed as threats to his absolute power. Not only was he King, but he was head of the Church of England as well, and he didn't intend to have his authority questioned by the Roman Catholic Church nor the Puritan/Protestant non-conformists. These differences would lead to Oliver Cromwell's Puritan Revolution of the 1640s, a Revolution in which King James' son, Charles I, was beheaded in 1649, the Glorious Revolution of 1688, and finally the American Revolution of 1776.

Government, according to Romans 13:1-4, is ordained by God. For a more detailed examination of this idea, please see Chapter 8, but suffice it to say here that Romans 13:1-4 is not teaching that God specifically sets in place particular governments, but that He has ordained the purpose of government. This does not jibe with the Calvinists' view of things nor even what many Christians believe about these verses. Nevertheless, I am convinced that the purpose of government is what is ordained by God, not the particular government, as so many believe. It must be remembered that

God is not addressing in His word people with no free-will. On the contrary, He is addressing people who will know that God has ordained government for their general welfare, and for this reason they are to willingly submit themselves to it.

At the same time, and this has been a much neglected subject among those who believe God specifically ordains particular governments and that men are duty bound to always obey such governments, the Bible makes it clear, I think, that a particular government is always the creation of men. For example, in 1 Peter 2:13-14, we are told to "Therefore submit yourselves to every ordinance of man for the Lord's sake, whether to the king as supreme, or to governors, as to those who are sent by him for the punishment of evildoers and for the praise of those who do good." It is the "every ordinance of man" that I want us to think about for a moment, for it is in this expression that we understand that although government has been ordained by God, particular governments, themselves, are always the creation of men.

Every Ordinance Of Man

Back in Chapter 1, when we discussed this expression, we learned that it was qualified, that is, we are not required to obey every ordinance of man no matter what, but only those things man-made governments have been delegated by God to exercise. Anything else puts us in the position of obeying God rather than man scenario, which is an idea we find articulated in Acts 4:19 and 5:29. However, the contrast between obey God rather than man clearly demonstrates that governments are definitely man-made, and because they are, they, like individuals, can conduct themselves contrary to what God has said. When they do, they lose their authority in those matters. In other words, there are things that must be rendered to Caesar as well as to God, but when Caesar attempts to command or legislate contrary to what God has commanded, Caesar or the State has no actual authority in such areas. Consequently, any disobedience of such commands is not rebellion at all, but holy disobedience.

The Greek word translated "ordinance" in the aforementioned phrase is *ktisis* and is, according to Strong's, "from *ktizo*; original *formation* (properly the act; by implication the thing, literally or figuratively):—building, creation, creature, ordinance." Thus, the very idea of such ordinances being a creation of man is built right into the words being used by the Holy Spirit. Every ordinance of man literally means every government/institution created by man. Particular governments, then, even particular forms of government, are instituted by men through their common consent, and not by direct divine decree. When this is understood, a whole different concept about the nature of human government is appreciated. It is this insight that motivated those subject to despotic government to realize that such institutions could be rightly resisted.

But How About God's Anointing Of Kings?

This is a good question and one that simply begs to be answered. Surprisingly, the Bible teaches that a man lawfully assumes the right only after being selected to do so by his fellow men. I say "surprisingly," not because such information ought to be a surprise for any serious student of the word, only that it usually is from those who have not spent much time studying to show themselves approved, as Scripture says we all should. But, as soon as this principle is fully understood and appreciated, it sheds its rays on the other areas of delegated authority we've already dealt with in Chapter 1, namely, the Home and the State. Although it doesn't hold true for children, and I'm sure this is because they simply do not have the ability to do so, the wife chooses the man to whose authority she will be submitting. The same is true of the Church, who collectively select/ordain those who will rule over them. Why, then, should we think it would be any different for the State?

The Consent Of The Governed

In Deuteronomy 17:5 and 2 Samuel 3:21, we learn that a man lawfully becomes ruler only after being selected by his fellow countrymen. His authority becomes effective when he enters into covenant with the people, according to 2 Samuel 5:1-3 and 1 Chronicles 11:3. God does not make one king directly. Although he had anointed David years before he ever became king, he was actually made king by the people.[15]

What's more, civil rulers do not have an absolute right to rule. In 1 Samuel 13:13-14, through His spokesman Samuel, God made this point crystal clear to Saul that because he acted foolishly and had not kept the commandments of God, he would be removed from power and replaced by another. From the New Testament, in places like 1 Peter 2:14 and Romans 13:4, we learn that civil rulers are commanded by God to honor those who do good and punish those who do evil. Their function is to uphold Justice and Righteousness in the nation for everyone, not to enrich themselves by preying on the very subjects they are commanded to serve and protect, as passages like Deuteronomy 17:18-19, Proverbs 31:5, 8-9, Psalm 72:12-14, and Jeremiah 22:3-4 point out. In other words, such govern "for the people," and not to heap to themselves even more power and wealth. Furthermore, if they neglect the first

---

15 See 2 Samuel 3:21; 5:1-3, and 1 Chronicles 11:3.

while engaging in the latter, then they lose their position as rulers, according to Proverbs 16:12 and 25:5.

The Case Of Athaliah: A Blueprint For Lawful Revolution

The Old Testament story of Athaliah is a prime example of the usurpation of a tyrant and how the rule of such a one can be remedied by lawful revolution. Israel's covenant with God was something the nation had entered into willingly. In other words, they were not forced to leave Egypt, enter Sinai, and there enter into a covenant relationship with God against their wills. They did so because they wanted to. (This is borne out by the fact that in the throes of revolt some of the people argued that it would have been better for them to have remained in Egypt and died than to be where they were. Some were even planning on returning.)[16]

In Exodus 19:1-8, the people agree to enter into covenant, saying in verse 8, "All that the Lord has spoken we will do." This they affirmed again in Exodus 24:3, where it says, "So Moses came and told the people all the words of the Lord and all the judgments. And all the people answered with one voice and said, 'All the words which the Lord has said we will do.'" Even after the trouble in the wilderness, a new generation renewed the covenant at Moab.[17] Then, after Moses' death, the people consented to Joshua's leadership.[18] Finally and very importantly, when it comes to considering the reign of Queen Athaliah, the covenant provided for male rulership only.[19]

---

16 See Deuteronomy 14:1-4 for one of these instances.
17 See Deuteronomy 29:1-21.
18 See Joshua 1:1-18.
19 See Deuteronomy 17:14-20.

All these facts are critical to interpreting the events surrounding the rise to power of Queen Athaliah and her subsequent overthrow. Summarizing these, Gary T. Amos wrote:

> *In this example, the form of government had been established by a covenant or compact. The person in the office violated the conditions of the covenant through acts of despotism and tyranny. She had no right to rule. The lower rulers and representatives of the people covenanted together to institute new government. Their revolution was forceful, but lawful. Joash was made king by the people when he entered into covenant with them.*[20]

Thus, the saga of Athaliah, a rebellious, murderous woman born of rebellious, murderous parents (viz., Ahab and Jezebel), serves as a blueprint for godly revolution that the Founding Fathers seemed to have followed meticulously. The procedure outlined above is easily discernable in the *Declaration of Independence*, which is reproduced in its entirety in the Appendix. If you have never read all of it, then I strongly urge you to do so, for when you do so, you can see for yourself just how scrupulously the Founding Fathers followed the aforementioned blueprint for revolution. None of this is to say that all the Founding Fathers had in mind exactly the account mentioned above, only that they were following a long list of thinkers and writers who had thought deeply about the Scriptural significance of such an account and how it applied to the circumstances of their day. I'm talking about men like Samuel Rutherford, who wrote *Lex Rex* or *The Law and the Prince* (1644) during the early stages of the English Civil War and John Locke, whose *Second Treatise of Government (1688)* so influenced the

---

[20] Amos, page 131.

political thought of the Colonies and the *Declaration of Independence,* all of which were critical of, and quite effectively so, the alleged Divine Right of Kings. These men had by various means arrived at a way of thinking about government that would, when fully embraced, cause the face of government to change dramatically in 1776, when our well-read Founding Fathers presented us with a form of government unparalleled in the history of mankind, a form to which man had actually been well-suited from the very beginning. Man does, in fact, have certain "unalienable rights" that are granted to him by his Creator. Therefore, government, which is ordained by God but created by man, must not attempt to interfere with such rights. It is, instead, duty-bound to protect them. When it doesn't, engaging instead in tyranny, despotism and arbitrary rule, it loses its right to govern.

Rutherford and Locke, both of whom were noted earlier, insisted that mere incompetence was not a reason for revolution. In other words, "[S]uch revolutions happen not upon every little mismanagement in public affairs."[21] The ruler must commit repeated acts of tyranny, that is, "a long train of abuses, prevarications, and artifices, all tending the same way" which "make the design visible to the people" that said ruler intends to destroy them and their land.[22] Again, a reading of the *Declaration of Independence* demonstrates that the Colonists' rejection of King George's rule was not a capricious act, but was undertaken only after a long list of abuses. Thus, the theory of revolution set forth in *Lex Rex* and the *Second Treatise* are the same and are based on Scriptural examples, like the one found in the saga of Athaliah and the circumstances surrounding the appointment of Jephthah as a prince over the people in

---

21 Locke, Second Treatise, page 126, section 225.
22 *Ibid.*

Judges 11:1-11, which Locke specifically referred to as an example of the people's right to choose those who would, in turn, rule over them, which serves as an example of the compact theory of government—a theory that said the people and ruler enter into a compact before God that binds both the ruler and the people to certain obligations and responsibilities.

If the ruler, then, fails in his part of the compact, then such failing is viewed as a material breach by which the ruler forfeits his right to rule. Tyranny, when it can be substantiated by repeated acts, is a material breach of the covenant or compact that exists between a ruler and those he rules. He can, then, be rightly deposed, not by riot and anarchy, but by the orderly exercise of duly constituted authorities who intercede on behalf of the people. That this is exactly what happened on July 4, 1776 is well established. Consequently, the American Revolution was not an act of rebellion against lawful authority, which would have been sinful, but resistance to and the ultimate casting off of a tyrant.

According to charges set forth in the *Declaration of Independence*, the king of England was a tyrant. This was established, it was claimed, by a series of tyrannical abuses: obstruction of justice; acts contrary to the public good; the suspension and impeding of legislatures; interfering with elections; corruption of the judiciary; wasting of the public and private wealth; the enforcement of martial law in time of peace; spying on the people; breaking charters; putting the government in the hands of those who had no right to rule; waging war against unarmed towns and cities, perpetrated repeated acts of theft, murder, and barbarity. In short, the king of England had denied the laws of nature, nature's God, and of England, repudiating its charters. He could, then, be lawfully deposed as a tyrant who had materially and repeatedly broken his promises.

That such was formal and public is self-evident. That such a *Declaration* was written by "representatives" of the people who, as lower magistrates, had assembled for the express purpose of inter-posing themselves between the king and those he sought to destroy cannot be denied. That in doing so, they appealed to the "Supreme Judge of the world" is another thing that cannot be denied. Based upon the evidence, and the motives of those involved, I believe it cannot be successfully denied that the American Revolution was, in fact, right and honorable in the sight of God. In other words, it was not just legal, but it was Biblical as well. The Biblical roots are "historically evident, logically compelling, and easily researchable."[23] Finally, although the Bible was not the only influence for its conception, I believe it is correct to say that without the Bible, the *Declaration of Independence* could have never been written.

That the United States of America is a nation that was built on certain eternal principles taught in God's word has continued to be its resounding legacy. As I have studied the history of its founding, it would be most difficult for me to think it happened due to some random collocation of atoms at a particular time and place—i.e., chance. Instead, I must think, like others before me, and I pray like others who will come after me, that America is what it is by the providential hand of Almighty God. In thinking such thoughts, I am reminded of what was said of the *U. S. Constitution,* a document that was constructed on the firm foundation of the *Declaration of Independence*—a document that was adopted on September 17, 1787, but was not formally ratified by two-thirds of the Colonies until June 21, 1788. About this document, the great British Prime Minister William Gladstone, a century later, said it was "the most wonderful work ever struck off at a given time by the brain

---

[23] Amos, page 150.

and purpose of man," an idea that seems to jibe nicely with George Washington's conclusion that "the event is the hand of God."[24]

In closing this chapter, I leave you with what Gary T. Amos said in the epilogue of his book, arguing that the American Revolution is really not over as long as there are those who do not believe that "all men are created equal." Writing of what he thinks to be today's consensus, he said:

> *Now, however, the Declaration's ideas are scoffed at by philosophers, misrepresented by historians, attacked by clergymen, ridiculed by law professors, held in contempt by power hungry politicians, and ignored by the people. As long as this continues, the American Revolution is not over.*[25]

---

[24] Gladstone's and Washington's quotes are from Hart, op. cit., page 329.
[25] Amos, page 170.

Chapter 4

The American Babylon: Our Home Away From Home

lthough I was just a junior in high school, I remember the presidential campaign of 1960 being one that focused on whether a Catholic president would be nothing less than a pawn of the Roman Catholic hierarchy. John F. Kennedy was young and popular, but a Roman Catholic, and a Roman Catholic had never before been elected to the presidency. In that day and age, anti-Catholicism ran high, particularly in the South where I grew up. Many of my fellow Christians were convinced that a Catholic president would not be good for the country, in that Catholicism requires a "dual loyalty," as Richard John Neuhaus has referred to it, something he had argued that involved "an allegiance to America *and* a prior allegiance to the [Roman Catholic] Church."[1]

JFK may have been a "good Catholic," as that term is used, but he seems to have been a much better politician. Consequently, he was able to convince enough of the American electorate that his role as the president would always trump any allegiance he had to the Catholic Church and its hierarchy. Consequently, he was elected the thirty-fifth President of the United States. In other words, he was able to convince the American people that his

---

1   "Our American Babylon," *First Things*, Dec. 25, 2006, pp. 23-28.

allegiance to the Catholic Church would take second seat to his secular responsibilities as President, and during the past half century the precedent that Kennedy set has been imbibed by other Catholics seeking political election or appointment. Some of the most recent of these are Justices Roberts and Alito, who both made it clear during their confirmation hearings that their religious beliefs would not impinge their decisions as Supreme Court Justices.

Hailed by many as a good thing, the pragmatic secularism[2] of Kennedy, Roberts, and Alito is clearly *in situ* (viz., in place) as the only acceptable philosophy to be granted permission in today's very secularized marketplace. Although the three men I've mentioned here were, and are, all Catholics, the "no religious convictions in the public square" syndrome so prevalent in 21st century America no longer reflects just some sort of anti-Catholicism, but touts the more general idea that religion—any religion—has no place in the secularized marketplace of ideas.

This kind of thinking is illustrated by an editorial that appeared in *The Atlanta Journal-Constitution*, entitled "Faith in Constitution is the Calling," written on behalf of the "editorial board" by David McNaughton, which said, in part:

> *John F. Kennedy put the question of a presidential candidate's religion in perspective when he noted the country has "far more critical issues to face."*

---

2 In its original sense, the term "secular" refers specifically to the natural—or real—world, if you will, distinct from the supernatural realm. However, there is another, completely different sense in which the term is used and this is captured by the suffix "ism," for *secularism* denotes a dedication to the natural, material world as opposed to the supernatural, and proclaims a kind of declaration of war against traditional religion, turning an otherwise proper distinction into a furious antagonism.

*That's as true today as it was in 1960, when Kennedy con-
fronted irrational suspicions that as a Catholic president he
would be controlled by the Vatican. Almost half a century
later, it's the Mormon religion of Republican Mitt Romney
that raises foolish suspicion in some quarters.*

*Romney's beliefs did not interfere with his official obliga-
tions when he was governor of Massachusetts. Nor would they
do so should he end up in the White House.*

*To assume otherwise is an insult to his faith and to the U.S.
Constitution, which states explicitly that "no religious test
shall ever be required as a qualification to any office of
trust."*[3]

The editorial closed by saying: "Two generations ago, Kennedy expressed the hope that 'religious intolerance will someday end.'
While that day has not yet come, that hope remains strong."[4]

This editorial by one of the most liberal newspapers in the
country, although ensconced in the deep South, is an example of
the anti-religious secularism that has become so prevalent in contemporary culture. Using the "no religious test" clause of Article
VI, section 3 of the *U.S. Constitution*, which was designed to prohibit duly-elected representatives of the people from being denied
political office because of some government-prescribed religious
test, the editorial board of *The Atlanta Journal-Constitution* argued
wrong-headedly, as well as a bit too sanctimoniously, that the general electorate have no right to even contemplate, much less question, the religious beliefs and values of a politician, even though
there is the possibility that such religiously held beliefs could influence his or her political decisions while in office. In their

3   Page A14, Friday, May 11, 2007.
4   *Ibid.*

description of those who would stoop to do such an underhanded thing, the editorial board referred to such suspicions as "irrational" and "foolish." But not only did the editorial board misrepresent the Framers' original intent, they clearly demonstrated their ignorance of what reasonable men and women know, almost intuitively, and that is that it is not wise to presume that all religions are created equal, as the events of 9/11 and their aftermath have so clearly demonstrated.[5]

Speaking Of "Foolish" And "Irrational"

While we're on the subject of the "foolish" and "irrational," was it not the liberal Left, along with its fellow travelers in the media elite who dubbed the Bush/Cheney/Ashcroft/Rove team as the "American Taliban"?[6] This is, of course, proof of the public schizophrenia taking place in our society over religion. For example, an intern dropping to her knees in the oval office to sexually service a lecherous president is defended as having nothing to do with the president's official performance of his duties and, therefore, nobody's business. Furthermore, when Clinton was impeached for lying under oath, claiming he "didn't have sex with that woman [viz., Monica Lewinsky]," he was let off the hook by liberal U.S. senators who refused to convict him because it just had to do with sex, and any man, some said, would lie under such

---

5   Please don't misunderstand what I'm saying here. I'm not saying such religions should not be granted constitutional privileges—they should, and they are!—only that it is a secularized prejudice that questions a citizen's prerogative to examine a candidate's religious allegiances and convictions in relation to the kind of decisions he or she might make in office.

6   Richard Rapaport, "The American Taliban," in the December 10, 2001 issue of *The San Francisco Chronicle*. Posted on the Internet at www.commondreams.org/views01/1210-07.htm.

circumstances. But when it was learned that George W. Bush dropped to his knees to pray every morning before he started his official workday in that very same oval office, it was viewed by the pundits with suspicion and scorn.

America Has Changed

Whether we like it or not, this is America at the beginning of the 21st century. But at the same time, it is America that has given shelter and sustenance to more New Testament Christians than any other country in the world. Even so, it is now clear that it is no longer the America it once was. Instead, contemporary America has become more pagan in its world view, and during this process, Biblical ethics have been increasingly unwelcomed in the public square. Consequently, the public morals of America, in too many instances, no longer derive from the Bible. Instead, they come mainly from the tenets of secular humanism. As such, the decisions of our judicial system have become more and more antithetical to Bible-based morality. Women, it was decided by the Supreme Court in 1973, now have a "right" to terminate the lives of their unborn infants at will upon any whim whatsoever. Anyone who disagrees with the "law of the land" is deemed to be "out of the mainstream" and "dangerous."

The highest court in the land has now decided that there is a "right" to practice homosexuality. Consequently, anyone who is deemed to have discriminated against homosexuals because of their "sexual orientation" is definitely "out of the mainstream" and "dangerous," and needs to be either prosecuted or treated (preferably both) for being, aghast, "homophobic." Some judges and public officials are already sanctioning the homosexual's right to "marry." I suspect it won't be all that long before such a travesty and mockery of God's ordained order will be the uniform "law of the land."

That the moral consensus in the United States of America has changed no fair-minded, right-thinking person can any longer deny. And as difficult as it may be for us to admit, it is, nevertheless, a fact that the republic our forefathers founded and nourished perished a long time ago. Consequently, this is no longer the country that made the Restoration Movement of Walter Scott, Thomas and Alexander Campbell, Barton W. Stone *et al.* possible. And because it is no longer that place, it is time for New Testament Christians to rethink their relationship *to* and *with* the government. This isn't going to be easy, but it is something I believe Christians who intend to be faithful to the Lord must be willing to do.

The "Most American" Of Churches

Because the Restoration Movement primarily started here, it is viewed by many as a uniquely American religion. In fact, in the *Handbook Of Denominations In The United States*, it is said of the Christian Church (Disciples of Christ), Christian Churches, and churches of Christ that "Among the half-dozen largest religious groups in the United States, [those making up the Restoration Movement] might be called the *most American*; it was born on the nineteenth century American frontier out of a deep concern for Christian unity."[7] Then, in Leroy Garrett's book, *The Stone-Campbell Movement: An Anecdotal History of Three Churches*, it is said about those who made up the Restoration Movement that "The heirs of the Movement now number upwards of four million,

---

[7] Frank S. Mead, fifth ed., 1970, pp. 64-65, emphasis mine—*AT*.

comprising the largest church (or churches) indigenous to this country."

However, those who make up conservative churches of Christ see themselves, and I believe rightly so, as being a part of that church to which the Lord added people on that first Pentecost after His resurrection and ascension into heaven.[8] But at the same time, it seems to me that there can be little doubt that we certainly owe some of *who* and *what* we are to the events known to history as the Restoration Movement and its American genesis.

Until Recently, Ours Has Been A Rather Comfortable Coexistence

Alexander Campbell (September 12, 1788 to March 4, 1866), the most prominent of the restorationists, standing, as he did, on the shoulders of some great thinkers before him (like Newton, Bacon, and Locke—especially Locke), was very much at ease with the separation of Church and State that was the American experiment—an experiment that was far different from the notion of the divine right of kings and the State church that had so dominated the European continent up to that time. Consequently, American churches of Christ, by and large, submitted themselves most willingly to the authority of the secular State. After all, the American form of government granted them the freedom of conscience and religion that their various European experiences had not provided.

Consequently, it was not hard for these Christians to render their wholehearted allegiance to the American system of government, for far from being a government to be feared, it offered them protection to worship God the way they thought best. And even

---

8   See Acts 2:47.

though many of the major Restoration leaders were conscientious objectors, rejecting military and police service because they believed such to be against Scripture, they found that the American system was most tolerant of their religious convictions, respecting their views so long as it could be demonstrated that they sincerely held them on religious grounds.

In turn, these same Restoration leaders taught their followers that they were scripturally obligated to obey the government and pay their taxes, which is clearly what the Bible teaches. Most of these leaders did not object to the government fighting wars in order to protect its citizens, only that such was something in which Christians ought not to be directly involved. But because being an American was so comfortable for most Christians, very little was ever said about holy disobedience.[9] But now, with the rise of secularism and its intrinsic tendency to exalt the State as the ultimate authority, it has become necessary to think about those times and circumstances when it is necessary for the faithful Christian to defy the State.

Defying The State

However, the idolized State does not take kindly the refusal of its subjects to obey its edicts. The Revelation 13 government of John's Apocalypse demanded worship and absolute obedience from its subjects. When Rome's citizens gave in to such demands by purchasing from the Concilia and, then, publicly burning

---

[9] Once again, what I mean by "holy disobedience" is this: Because God never granted the State unquestioned, absolute power, there are times when its demands and laws must be rejected. In other words, and as Peter and the other apostles taught, there are times when the faithful Christian must obey God rather than men (cf. Acts 5:29).

incense to Caesar as God, they were afforded all the "rights" of Roman citizenship. These included the free handouts Rome provided its citizens, along with permission to join and remain in the various work guilds, without which it would be very difficult to support oneself and family. But when its recalcitrant citizens refused to worship and obey (viz., burn a little incense to Caesar), they were severely punished, sometimes even to the point of death.

What this all means is that there is an immense difference between the way Rome treated its citizens in ancient times and the way the United States of America has traditionally interacted with its people. Instead of persecuting Christians as Rome did, America has protected and carefully guarded the right of its citizens to worship God as they deem appropriate. As a result, American Christians, basking in the freedom that many governments around the world have done their best to extinguish, have thought it almost unthinkable that they should engage in any form of disobedience toward the State, whether it be the local, state, or federal governments. The thesis of this book is that it is high time for us to rethink this relationship, along with its many attendant issues.

Thus, in the chapter that follows I'll direct your attention specifically to the unwholesome affect the modern, idolized State is having on New Testament Christians.

Chapter 5

Marriage, Divorce, And Remarriage As Viewed By The Christian, The State, And The Church: The Issue Personified

When it comes to the Christian's relationship with the State, issues surrounding marriage, divorce, and remarriage (hereafter referred to as MDR) serve as the personification of the difficult and controversial question of when to obey or disobey the government. I hope these issues will become clearer before you finish this book.

As was noted in the dedication, MDR is a subject my wife and I take very seriously. Our marriage of forty-three years is, I believe, an ample demonstration of this point. I think this needs to be said for, as you will learn, those who take the position on MDR that I will be defending are frequently charged with having a very low view of marriage. I can't speak for all, of course, but from my standpoint, I categorically deny such a charge. In fact, my view regarding the sanctity of marriage is so strong (some will, no doubt, describe it as draconian) that I believe it is *not only permissible* for the State to inflict capital punishment for adultery, so long as such procedures are carried out commensurate with Justice and Righteousness, *but also desirable*. And if such a view were actually reflected in American society, you could be certain we would not be having the MDR problem we're experiencing in our country, and in the church. So, whatever you might think about my position on MDR, if you are a fairminded person, you will be hard-pressed to think of it as somehow holding the sanctity of marriage in low esteem.

But I really said all that to say this: *There is a prevalent doctrinal point of view that says the "innocent party," which is implied from Jesus' statements in Matthew 5:32 and 19:9, when legally, but not scripturally, divorced by his or her mate is, for the lifetime of that mate, forever locked into a state of celibacy, and that this remains true even after the one doing the unscriptural "putting away" subsequently commits adultery.* Although this view appears to be held by many, perhaps even most, of my brethren, I view it as a completely unscriptural and totally wrong-headed position that binds where God hasn't bound and, in the process, commits a terrible injustice against the only one who, by God's permission, has been given leave to put an adulterous mate away for fornication and marry again without sin.

Now, it is certainly true that when two people are divorced for some reason other than fornication, each must remain "unmarried" or else be reconciled to his or her mate, as Paul instructed in 1 Corinthians 7:11. If either is joined to another sexually, he or she would be committing adultery, according to Matthew 5:32 and 19:9. There is no doubt in my mind that this is precisely what Jesus taught in these passages. But to argue, as many do, that when the one who obtained the unscriptural divorce goes out and commits adultery, the innocent party has no recourse but to remain celibate, runs totally contrary to the Lord's teaching—namely, *the only one permitted to put a mate away and marry again, without sin, is the innocent party who puts his or her mate away "for fornication".*

Thus, to prohibit a sinned against mate from scripturally putting away a fornicating partner, even though the sinful partner has already obtained a legal, but totally unscriptural, divorce, is to prohibit the very thing for which the Lord designed the exception clause in the first place.

The So-Called Sin Of "Mental Divorce"

But because I believe this principle remains true even after a totally legal, but absolutely unscriptural, divorce, I have been labeled a "mental divorcer." However, I do not believe this label accurately identifies my position and I personally reject it. I believe its use, whether intentional or not, functions to prejudice others as to what I actually believe, teach and practice on this subject. Nonetheless, for the sake of making a defense of my position and then showing how it impacts the Christian and the State, I will concede, for the sake of argument, that it is precisely this so-called and much-maligned "Mental Divorce" position that I'll be defending in this chapter and throughout the rest of this book.

Rejecting The Tactics Of Some

This means that I'll not be trying to deflect the implications of my position by claiming, as some do, that "we" all believe the same doctrine (viz., one man, one woman, for life, except for fornication), and that it is only in the application of this doctrine that we have some disagreements and, further, that such disagreements aren't really serious enough to affect fellowship. Nor will I stoop to arguing that when one presses me to scripturally defend my position, he is somehow guilty of sowing discord among brethren and should, himself, be reprimanded.

Such tactics are totally carnal and ought not to be weapons in the Christian's arsenal. Besides, what one understands to be a biblical doctrine is defined by his interpretation of a particular passage (or passages) which is, in turn, manifested by the specific application he makes of said passages or passage. Thus, for one to argue that we all agree on what the Bible says, just not its application, and that this should not impinge upon fellowship, is nothing but another example of that ol' "why can't we all just get along" philosophy of the infamous Rodney King dressed up in the nonsensical garb of religious mumbo-jumbo.

A Very Serious Subject

The matter before us is not just some insignificant personal scruple that can be tolerated by others in the community of believers. Consequently, the local church will have to decide whether or not to fellowship one who has exercised himself in light of the doctrine I am here defending. Moreover, one who preaches and teaches on this subject, as I have done, is more than likely to find himself identified as a "false teacher." Therefore, this subject is not something that can be swept under the rug and ignored, as some seem disposed to do.

But This Is Not About Fellowship, Per Se

But as important as it is to acknowledge the fellowship implications of this doctrine and to deal with them honestly and forthrightly, I wish to make it clear that fellowship, *per se*, is not the object of this study. What some individual or local congregation will or will not fellowship is always important, but such is not my direct concern here. My task, as I see it at this juncture, is to openly and honestly defend what I believe to be the truth on this subject—a truth I believe to have been much maligned, misunderstood and, in some cases, even misrepresented.

It Is Just As Wrong To Bind As It Is To Loose

But before going any further, I want to make it perfectly clear—even though I briefly touched on this in the previous chapter—that I believe the Bible teaches it is wrong to loose where God hasn't loosed.[1] Thinking this to be exactly what my position does, some have not hesitated to call it "heresy." Now, I realize this term can be simply emotive (i.e., someone just viscerally reacting to a position with which he strongly disagrees), but there remains a real biblical sense in which this term may be used. Consequently, I want all who read here to know that I understand both the serious nature and ramifications of this issue. If my position is wrong, then I just may be a heretic. At the same time, I want to remind everyone that there's a flip side to this coin which must be fully understood if meaningful dialogue is to occur—that is, *it is just as wrong to bind where God hasn't bound as it is to loose where He hasn't loosed*.

This means that one may well be binding where God hasn't bound when he argues that when one's scripturally bound mate commits fornication, the innocent party has no right to divorce the guilty mate and marry again, without sin, when the guilty party has already secured a legal divorce for some reason other than fornication. So, with the reminder that what is good for the goose is good also for the gander, all should be constrained to be circumspect, and this no matter what position they hold. Because this subject is so serious, and because it impacts individual Christians, as well as local churches, it simply cannot be ignored.

I think it helpful just here to be reminded that Jesus frequently found Himself confronted, challenged and charged by those holding the "majority opinion." His teaching on various scriptures

---

1   See Revelation 22:18-19.

often clashed with the "tradition of the elders."[2] Thus, just because a position is in the minority does not automatically mean it is wrong. Of course, unlike Jesus, I do not have perfect understanding of all things, and the fact that many of my brethren disagree with me on this issue has given me cause to seriously reflect on what they are saying. So far, none of their arguments have been convincing.

I Remain Open To Being Taught

While I would like to be seen as a humble, but confident, proclaimer of what I believe the Bible teaches on this subject, I also want to be seen as a sincere and eager listener. Therefore, I remain open to being taught on this, or any other, subject. But because I have found my position so frequently misunderstood and misrepresented, I believe it necessary to offer the following defense—a defense I sincerely believe to be totally consistent with "the faith which was once and for all delivered to the saints."[3] But as strange as it may sound, I do this not so much to actually defend my position, which I am always happy to do, but to specifically illustrate how this issue so aptly demonstrates the tension that exists between the Christian and the State. Although there are certainly other issues that would have done so, I can't think of one that would do so better.

As noted previously, it has been asserted that the position I hold on MDR somehow demonstrates a low view of marriage. Those who say so claim it is, in fact, "in violation of what the Bible teaches and is pernicious in its consequences." Accordingly, it is

---

2   Matthew 5:2; Mark 7:1-8.
3   Jude 3.

claimed that it is a position "born not of sound exegesis but of a desire to circumvent the Lord's teachings."[4] I have no reason to believe that the one who actually wrote the above quoted words had me specifically in mind, even though he and I have discussed this issue on more than one occasion. Yet, there can be no doubt that those who hold the doctrine I am here defending were, indeed, the objects of these remarks. In taking exception to but only one thing he wrote, I want to make it clear that I have no problem with what was said except his uncalled-for assertion that my position is "born...of a desire to circumvent the Lord's teaching." His attempt to assign an evil motive to my position is a subject that I, quite frankly, don't think my critic is in any position to pass judgment on. Furthermore, if it could be demonstrated that such was, in fact, my motive for taking the "Mental Divorce" position, and I assure you it isn't, this alone would make me guilty of sin, would it not? Thus, such a remark unfairly taints with sin all who hold the "Mental Divorce" position, and this before any attempt is made to scripturally refute it. It is unfortunate that such tactics are all too frequently exhibited in the rhetoric of such critics. Such may be an effective debate technique, at least in some people's minds, but it does nothing to scripturally refute the position.

I believe it is perfectly legitimate to argue (and then attempt to scripturally prove) that a position is "in violation of what the Bible teaches" and, therefore, "pernicious in its consequences." I believe it is even valid to argue (and then attempt to prove) that a position is "born not of sound exegesis." But it is clearly not right to judge the motives of another's heart without being able to prove it. The other charges I can attempt to refute by an appeal to God's word, but the only defense I have to the latter charge is that I don't

---

4   I have not given the documentation for this citation, as I do not wish to call attention to the personalities involved.

believe it is true. In this case, it would just be my word against his, and even if you believed me, this would still be a somewhat "iffy" proposition, as the Bible says, "The heart is deceitful above all things, and desperately wicked; who can know it?"[5]

I point this out to say this: If a discussion of this, or any other, subject can be kept on the level of a Bible study, dispensing with unwarranted and ungodly character assassination and personal invective, there is hope that those in error on this subject, no matter what side they're on, will learn the truth and be converted. With this said, permit me to state unequivocally, and as succinctly as I know how, my basic hermeneutic (i.e., my way of interpreting the Scriptures):

> *I believe it is possible to discover the true meaning of a given text of Scripture by following the rules of grammar and syntax combined with the literary context and style of the passage and the historical, cultural context of the author. I believe there can be only one correct interpretation of a text which faithfully expounds what the author was saying, and this means that all other interpretations are wrong.*

I think most who disagree with me on MDR hold to the same hermeneutic. Therefore, I ask only that they be willing to abide by the same rules of interpretation they seek to impose on others. If there is something wrong with my basic hermeneutic or my various exegeses, I believe those who disagree with me have every right to point this out. But please note that such a method has consequences. By this, I mean it is not permissible for those who disagree with me to just make the claim there are flaws in my interpretation. Instead, they are under obligation to prove it. This is only

---

5 Jeremiah 17:9.

right and honorable and no one on either side of this issue ought to get huffy about it, as this naturally and honestly provides a stage for meaningful dialogue.

The Regulator Of MDR Is God, Not Man

It is God, not man, who ordained marriage.[6] It is God, not man, who authorized divorce for fornication.[7] And it was God, not man, who set the conditions for one to remarry without sin.[8] When we keep these truths firmly entrenched in our minds, then what the laws of men permit or forbid are not nearly as important as what God forbids and permits.

This does not mean that marriage is a church "sacrament," as the Roman Catholics claim. Nor does it mean that marriage is a church "ordinance," as many Protestants assert. The establishment of Christ's church was yet many years in the future when the events of Genesis 2:24 took place. This means that when two people who have the God-given right to marry are married, regardless of who or what they are religiously, it is God who joins them together.[9] In other words, marriage is a creation mandate. Thus, all men and women are amenable to it. The fact that most of God's creation no longer know this is true is manifested in the cavalier way many today view marriage. Nevertheless, such callousness does not change reality. When two people who have a God-given right to marry are married, God yokes them together. This means, among other things, that they are no longer two, but "one flesh."[10]

---

6 See Genesis 2:24.
7 See Matthew 5:32 and 19:9.
8 See Deuteronomy 24:1; Matthew 5:32; 19:9.
9 See Matthew 19:6b.
10 Matthew 19:6a.

Without God's yoking, there can be no "one flesh" relationship, and this remains the truth whether anyone believes it or not.

What Do I Mean By "Creation Mandate"?

By *creation mandate*, I'm referring to those things men and women are compelled to do because they are, in fact, creatures of God, made in His image. These things do not change over time and cover the whole breadth of God's interaction with man, be it the Patriarchal, Mosaical, or Christian dispensations. To give you an example of what I am talking about, let's first look at something other than marriage, like the creation mandate against murder.

In Genesis 9:6, God said, "Whoever sheds man's blood, by man his blood shall be shed: for in the image of God He made man." Although there are some today who look upon this statement as utterly barbaric, most have recognized this principle as the foundation of civilized society. Man is unique in that he is made in God's image, and his "right to life" must not be interfered with by any other creature. If this principle is broken and a man is murdered, then the murderer must, consistent with Justice and Righteousness, be put to death.[11] This moral regulation stands apart from the Law of Moses given at Sinai and has no more been rescinded than the fact that man is made in God's image. As Genesis 9:6 makes clear, God has universally legislated against murder.

Therefore, it should not surprise us to see this principle incorporated into the Law of Moses, and this is exactly what we see. In Exodus 20:13, the sixth commandment of the Decalogue says, "You shall not murder." Under the Mosaical covenant, the murderer was to be put to death. If the murderer was not executed, the

---

[11] See Genesis 9:5-6.

land was defiled.[12] Clearly, then, the God of the Old Testament not only believed in capital punishment, He demanded it.

Although God's attitude about capital punishment during the Patriarchal and Mosaical covenants cannot be misunderstood, some are convinced He changed His mind in the New Testament. According to some, capital punishment is much too cruel a penalty to be condoned by the meek and humble Jesus. According to yet others, and I'm speaking here of those who consider themselves to be enlightened humanists, the God of the Old Testament was the product of a primitive people; therefore, He was represented as a vengeful and barbaric deity. But as mankind became more "civilized," they claim, a more loving, caring, and forgiving deity has been developed. According to these humanistic theologians and materialistic elitists, the "god" (notice the little "g") of the New Testament is but a "mellowed-out" caricature of the Old Testament's deity.

But to the contrary, the Bible makes it clear that the God of the Old Testament and the God of the New Testament are one and the same. In truth, the God who has revealed Himself throughout all history has not changed in any of His characteristics or attributes.[13]

In the New Testament, Jesus, who was none other than God incarnate,[14] said, "You shall not murder."[15] This, of course, proved what we should, by now, already intuitively know, and this is that God's moral prohibition against murder has not changed. Murder has been, is, and always will be, wrong, and the Bible consistently portrays it this way.

---

12 Numbers 35:30-33.
13 See Malachi 3:6; Jas. 1:17.
14 See John 1:1-17.
15 Matthew 19:18.

As long as man is made in the image of God, murder will be wrong and capital punishment for the murderer will be right. Everyone, and especially those who claim to be following Jesus, should know God's moral code forbids murder.[16] On this truth there can be no legitimate disagreement. The prohibition against murder, then, is a creation mandate enforceable in every dispensation and in every situation.

In other words, murder is always wrong and capital punishment for the murderer, when carried out consistent with Justice and Righteousness, is always right. In this regard, it is important to note that it was Paul, an inspired apostle, who said if he had done anything worthy of death, he refused "not to die."[17] And it was God Himself who gave the State the power of the sword—namely, the right to exercise capital punishment.[18]

Likewise, marriage, which is another of God's creation mandates, is the only place where man can engage in sexual intercourse without sin.[19] Therefore, as long as the creation mandate of marriage is in force, fornication and adultery will be wrong. This was true under the Patriarchal and Mosaical periods, and it is true today in the Christian age. The Lord made it clear in Matthew 19:4-9 that what God has said about MDR is a mandate that all mankind must honor (viz., one man, one woman, for life, except for fornication). Consequently, I do not believe this mandate has changed one *iota* since it was instituted by God at the beginning.

Nevertheless, many New Testament Christians, perhaps even most, believe that what Jesus taught in Matthew 19:4-9 and 5:31-32 was a new exception designed just for the New Testament age.

---

16 See Romans 13:9; 1 Peter 4:15; 1 John 3:15.
17 Acts 25:11.
18 See Romans 13:1-4.
19 See Proverbs 5:15-23; Hebrews 13:4.

Such an interpretation has led some to teach that non-Christians are not amenable to the Lord's teaching in these passages. Consequently, it is necessary for me to spend some time demonstrating why I believe what Jesus taught during His earthly ministry was what had been the truth on this subject all along. This, then, is the issue to be addressed in the next chapter.

Chapter 6

From A Biblical Point Of View, What Exactly Is Marriage, Divorce, And Remarriage?: An Examination Of God's Tamper-Proof Rules

I n Matthew 19:4-9, Jesus was not instituting a new set of rules for MDR. Instead, He was reminding the Jews of what MDR *had been* (Patriarchal age), *was* (Mosaical age), and *always would be* (New Testament age). From the very beginning, marriage was a one man, one woman, relationship that was intended to last for a lifetime. Therefore, if either of the parties to a God-ordained marriage obtained a divorce, except it be for the cause of fornication, and was joined to another, adultery would always be the result. Although there is nothing recorded during the Patriarchal age concerning the actual remedy available to the innocent party, the implication, according to Jesus' commentary in Matthew 19:4-9, is that it was death for the guilty party. Death for the guilty party, when exercised, would have allowed the innocent member to remarry without sin, for the guilty party would be dead, and one is only bound by the law, according to the apostle Paul, as long as one's mate is alive.[1] Therefore, when one's mate dies, he or she is at

---

1   See Romans 7:2, 3; 1 Corinthians 7:39.

liberty to be married to another without sin. This is consistent with the one man, one woman for life mandate that Jesus spoke of in Matthew 19:4-6.

Of course, mankind has never been too keen on honoring God's marriage mandate. It was Lamech (of Cain's lineage) who is recorded as the first man in the Bible with multiple wives.[2] Later, during the Mosaical age, God instructed the king who would be righteous not to "multiply wives for himself."[3] Of course, in Exodus 20:14, God specifically prohibited adultery, prescribing death as the penalty, according to Leviticus 20:10. This, along with Jesus' commentary in Matthew 19:4-9, gives credence to the idea that physical death was always the temporal penalty for adultery. As I've already said, it is safe to say that if this penalty were being imposed by civil authorities today, we wouldn't be having the problem with MDR that's so prevalent in our culture and, now, in the church of our Lord.

But What About That "Certificate Of Divorce" During The Mosaical Age?

In Deuteronomy 24:1-4, Moses, with God's permission, permitted the Israelites to divorce their wives for "uncleanness." This was accomplished by the husband writing a certificate of divorcement and putting it in his wife's hand. According to Jesus' commentary on this passage in Matthew 19:8-9, I believe the "some uncleanness" was, necessarily, fornication (viz., adultery). Some are quick to say that this interpretation can't be correct because adultery during the Mosaical age was punishable by death. Yes,

---

2 See Genesis 4:19.
3 Deuteronomy 17:17.

this is what God had commanded, but because of the "hardness of [their] hearts" they were not going to consistently and judiciously execute adulterers for their crimes. That this is undoubtedly the case is demonstrated by the fact that if the Israelites had been willing to obey the Lord and judiciously execute adulterers, there would have been no need for Moses to have "permitted" a writing of divorce.

Therefore, giving a writing of divorcement appears to have been enacted to avert a greater evil, for without such legislation a man might unmercifully treat a wife in whom he found "some uncleanness," even to the point of permanently injuring or killing her. "This is ridiculous," some say, "as death was the Law's punishment for adultery." Yes, it was, but because of the hardened hearts of the Jews, it was not going to be righteously carried out. Even today, adulterers still deserve death, but there are very few courts [none in this country], and perhaps fewer Christians, who would seek to exact such a "harsh" punishment. Why? Because of the hardness of our hearts, of course. We simply do not see adultery, even the kind that takes place in our hearts, as the horrendous sin it really is, for many who call themselves after Christ attempt to justify the harboring of such unholy desires as being perfectly human and, therefore, natural.

Only when we see this sin as God sees it will we be able to understand there has always been only one reason given by God to sever the divinely ordained relationship of marriage, and that is adultery. The God-ordained penalty is death. [Again, if civil authorities were willing to enforce God's MDR mandate, we would not be having a MDR problem today in our culture and in the church. But because capital punishment requires a certain judicial procedure in order to ensure that justice will be done, just like it did for the Jews in Moses' day, and because of our own hardness of hearts today, just like the Jews, few would be willing to pursue such an effort.] Consequently, because the sinned against party was not permitted by God's law to take justice into his own hands, he was, instead, to write her a "certificate of divorce," and "put it in her hand" before sending her away. To beat her, or in any other way mistreat her, was forbidden and this, because of the hardness of men's hearts, would be the sinned against mate's only remedy.

But many of the Jews had wrongly interpreted Deuteronomy 24:1-4 to be saying a man could put his mate away "for just any reason."[4] They were wrong, and Jesus emphatically said so. Therefore, I find it more than just a little ironic that many Christians today make the Jews' same mistake in their interpretation of Deuteronomy 24:1-4. The scribes and Pharisees wrongly taught and believed that a certificate of divorce, no matter what the cause, dissolved the marriage in the eyes of God. Consequently, they taught that a Jewish man was permitted by Moses to put his wife away and marry another whenever, and for whatever reason, he wanted. They were wrong on both accounts. The end result was not just "legalized divorce," but "legalized adultery," as well.

Legalized Divorce & Adultery

What do I mean by "legalized divorce"? Simply this: Any divorce that is not scriptural but is, nevertheless, sanctioned by the State. By "not scriptural," I mean any divorce that is not "for fornication." And what do I mean by the term "legalized adultery"? Only this: Any "marriage" sanctioned by man that God identifies as adulterous. In fact, "legalized divorce" and "legalized adultery" are exactly the positions touted by those who followed the ancient Jewish school of Hillel, declaring it a sufficient cause for divorce if

---

4   Matthew 19:3.

the wife had spoiled her husband's dinner. The Jewish historian, Flavius Josephus, himself a two-time divorcé, had this to say about it:

> *He that desires to be divorced from his wife for any cause whatsoever (and many such causes happen among men), let him in writing give assurance that he will never use her again as his wife any more; for by this means she may be at liberty to marry another husband, although before this bill of divorce be given, she is not permitted so to do.*[5]

It was just this kind of wrong-headed thinking that Jesus was attempting to correct.[6] In truth, Moses did not permit divorce and remarriage for "just any cause"—the only cause then and now is "unchastity" or fornication. Consequently, Jesus was not teaching something new and revolutionary with his MDR teaching in the Sermon on the Mount. Instead, He was teaching MDR the way it had always been viewed in God's sight: *namely, one man, one woman, for life.* However, when the hardness of men's hearts prevents the death penalty from being carried out for adultery, the Lord permits a divorce "for fornication," which is the kind of divorce I'm referring to when I use the term "scriptural divorce."

God's Rules Are As Binding Today As They Ever Were

God's rules concerning a scriptural divorce are as binding today as they were during the Mosaical period, and I have every reason to believe they were in force during Patriarchal times, as well.

---

5 *Antiquities*, IV, viii, 23.
6 In all fairness, there was another school, that of Shammai, that rightfully held that a man could not divorce his wife except for some "unchastity," but such was, unfortunately, the *minority* opinion.

In other words, if the one man, one woman, for life principle, coupled with permission to put one's mate away for fornication whenever the hardness of men's hearts prevents the death penalty from being exercised, does not predicate the death sentence for adultery, then I am at a complete loss to know just how one is to arrive at a necessary conclusion about anything.

Moreover, if the death penalty were actually in play for adultery, one would be very careful about accusing his or her mate of that offense. (Remember that both males and females were to be put to death for adultery according to Leviticus 10:20.) Therefore, in a culture where the death penalty was not going to be consistently carried out, and the Lord knew this would shamefully be the case with the Israelites, the Lord permitted a scriptural putting away for fornication. But because it would be the tendency of hard-hearted people to misuse and misinterpret the significance of this permission, using it to divorce their mates "for just any reason,"[7] God stipulated, through Moses, that when one's mate was sent away, the divorced mate could not be taken back when she subsequently married someone else, even if the put away mate's next "husband" died. From these instructions, several things appear evident: (1) When the death penalty is being enforced and the accused mate is convicted and executed, the companionship and comfort provided by the executed mate could never be retrieved. (2) In lieu of the death penalty, divorcing a mate for fornication should not provide the innocent with benefits he or she could not enjoy if the death penalty were in force. (3) Before the put away mate was "married" to someone else (Jesus called such a marriage "adultery"), the innocent mate could reconcile with the guilty partner based upon her repentance, and do so without sinning.

---

7 Matthew 19:3.

Fornicator Not Released

According to the doctrine of Christ, the only marriage partner permitted to marry again is the one whose mate is dead or has divorced his or her mate for fornication. This means the mate put away for fornication, or for some reason other than fornication, commits adultery when he or she "marries" another. Consequently, I believe it is reasonable to conclude that God implemented the restrictive you-can't-take-her-back clause of Deuteronomy 24:4 to militate against the legalized marriages the Jews would be inclined to engage in due to the hardness of their hearts—legalized marriages that would, in fact, be nothing less than legalized adultery. Now, if my reasoning here is not sound, then please be so kind as to point this out and demonstrate why. (Notice, also, that I see no need to argue that only men were permitted to put a mate away under the law of Moses, as many do. In fact, God permitted either the man or the woman to put one's mate away for fornication, just as either was able to charge a mate with adultery according to Leviticus 20:10.)

Hence, based on what Jesus said about marriage from the very beginning and what Moses said about a "certificate of divorce," coupled with Jesus' commentary on all this, I believe the MDR mandate of one man, one woman, for life, except for fornication, was in force from the very beginning and is, therefore, a mandate to which all are amenable. This means that Jesus' teaching on MDR is not just obligatory for New Testament Christians, as some teach; but is, instead, universal in nature and something all are subject to.

The question is sometimes asked, "If a civil divorce for some reason other than fornication is not really the divorce Jesus was talking about in Matthew 5:32 and 19:9, then how is it possible for man to actually 'put asunder' what God has joined together?"

First, there are two kinds of divorce under discussion in these verses. One divorce is "for fornication" (this is what I'm calling a "scriptural divorce") and the other is "for just any cause" (this is what I'm calling "legalized divorce"). By executing the latter, man can, and does, "put asunder" what God has joined together, but when he does so, he is engaged in sin.[8] It would have been nonsensical for Jesus to say that man could, in fact, put asunder what God had joined together, if it was not actually *possible* for man to do so. Consequently, I do not teach that man cannot put asunder what God has joined together—*he can and he does*. What I teach is that man ought not to put asunder what God has joined together, and when he does, there are serious, sometimes terrible, consequences that ensue.

Because God is an integral part of the covenant made between the two marriage partners, any "putting asunder" without fornication on the part of one of the partners is not permitted by God, and would be what I'm calling an "unscriptural [read 'legalized'] divorce." In such cases, God does not release—I repeat, *does not release*—either party from the "bond" He has placed them under. What this means is that the Bible teaches it is possible to be legally (viz., in the sight of man) divorced, but still bound in God's sight. Therefore, it is possible, as is often the case, that a couple may be "legally divorced" without being "scripturally divorced." Under such circumstances, both parties are still bound. If this is not a scriptural conclusion, then one is obligated to point this out and demonstrate why. However, if my exegesis is correct, then we are, in all probability, in general agreement up to this point. Where, then, do we begin to disagree? We disagree, I think, over just what it is that constitutes a scriptural, God-ordained marriage. Some of

---

8 See Matthew 19:6.

you may be thinking, "No, Allan, it's not what constitutes a scriptural, God-ordained marriage that's the problem; the problem is what constitutes a divorce." Well, then, bear with me for a moment as I elaborate on this.

What, Then, Is A Scriptural, God-Ordained Marriage?

A scriptural, God-ordained marriage is a covenantal relationship between (1) a man and (2) a woman, both of whom have permission from God to be married, and (3) God Himself. In other words, if scriptural, the couple is "joined together" (i.e., scripturally married, yoked, bound, *et cetera*) by God Himself. If this isn't true, then someone is going to have to tell me what Matthew 19:6 is really saying. If, however, my interpretation is correct, then the "one flesh" relationship into which God joins the two parties of a scriptural, God-ordained marriage is not just the physical relationship. *Actually, there is much more to marriage than this.* I emphasize this because the fact that marriage is more than a physical relationship is critical to understanding the argument I'll be making throughout this study. In point of fact, the physical relationship can be—and usually is—broken by an unscriptural (i.e., "legalized") divorce. Even so, and here's the critical point, in such cases *God does not release either of the parties from the marriage bond.* Therefore, if either of the divorced persons joined him- or herself to another, adultery would be the result.

Yet, someone at this juncture may be obliged to ask, "Is marriage something that can be kept private?" No, not normally; but it must be remembered that Adam and Eve, who are the human models for marriage, did not perform their oaths/vows before other human beings. The only "witness" was God Himself,[9] and it must be remembered that it was the Lord God who "brought [the woman] to the man."[10] Commenting on this phrase, the *Pulpit Commentary* says, "I.e. led, conducted, and presented her to Adam." Then quoting Bush in the English edition of *The Book of Genesis*, London, 1859, it says, "The word implies the solemn bestowment of her in the bonds of the marriage covenant, which is hence called the covenant of God (Prov. ii. 17); implying that He [God] is the Author of this sacred institution." I don't think there's a Christian who would argue that Adam and Eve were not really married, and if not, it must be acknowledged that the circumstances and situations in which a couple find themselves may impinge on what we normally believe to be the trappings of a scriptural, God-ordained marriage.

Ideally, Three Things Seem To Be Necessary

Having said all this, and because marriage is, in fact, a covenant,[11] it appears reasonable that there are, ideally, three things required for a scriptural, God-ordained marriage to occur, and please keep in mind that I am emphasizing "ideally" here: (1) a statement of intent, (2) an oath (or vow) by each to observe the terms of the covenant, and (3) some form of ratification of the covenant by a public, culturally accepted act, usually coincident with the oath itself. God, of course, is not only a witness to all this, as has already been pointed out, He is actually the One who joins the couple together.[12] When this occurs, an irrevocable bond yokes the two,

---

9   See Malachi 2:14.
10 Genesis 2:22b.
11 See Malachi 2:14.
12 See Genesis 2:22b; Matthew 19:6.

making them, according to Matthew 19:6, "one flesh." The only exception to this is when one of the mates commits fornication. Even then, the bond, with all its duties and obligations, remains intact. The innocent party, according to Deuteronomy 24:1, Matthew 5:32, and Matthew 19:9, may then exercise his or her right to put away (i.e., scripturally divorce) the guilty mate. However, there may be reasons for not dissolving the marriage—reasons in which repentance, mercy, and prudence play important parts. But, and here's another extremely important point, when the innocent party exercises his or her right to put a guilty mate away, *the only one released from the bond is the innocent party.* Therefore, it is only the innocent party who is free to marry again without committing adultery.

Some have argued that this just doesn't seem right, in that if the innocent party is released from the obligations of the bond, then the guilty party should be released as well. This, however, is not what the Bible teaches, and such thinking represents faulty, humanistic reasoning.[13] There is, in fact, absolutely nothing in the Bible by way of a direct statement, approved example, or necessary inference that permits the guilty party to marry again without sin.

In Galatians 3:15, the apostle Paul said, "Though it is only a man's covenant, yet if it is confirmed, no one annuls or adds to it." The English word "confirmed" is from the Greek *kuroo*, which, according to *Strong's*, means "to make authoritative, i.e. ratify." Consequently, when a contract, covenant, will, testament, or agreement is made between two parties, it cannot be either annulled (i.e., "set aside," "despised," or "brought to naught") or added to without serious consequences. This is especially true

---

13 By "humanistic reasoning," I simply mean reason uninformed by Scripture.

when God is a witness of, as well as a party to, the covenant. Therefore, the consequences of "setting aside" or "putting asunder" one's obligations and responsibilities under the marriage covenant presents only one of two possibilities: (1) the opportunity of being reconciled to one's "husband" (or "wife") through repentance (an opportunity that can only be extended through the mercy of the one sinned against), or (2) the obligation to remain "unmarried" for the rest of one's life.[14] If you agree with me on this, and I believe most who read here will do so, it is time to enter the thorny territory of Church-State issues, an area that can be more like the "Twilight Zone" than any other aspect of this study.

---

[14] See 1 Corinthians 7:11.

Chapter 7

The "Twilight Zone" Of Church-State Issues

But "Why," you might ask, "is it necessary to walk this prickly Church-State territory?" Because, those who disagree with me argue that in order for a marriage covenant to be valid, there must be (1) a statement of intent, (2) an oath (or vow) by each of the parties to observe the terms of the agreement, and (3) the formal ratification of the covenant by some external act.[1] They further argue that the particular sign of ratification in our society (speaking of the United States) is a "legal formality." Finally, it is said, quite emphatically, that a "relationship without the agreement, vows, and ratification is not a marriage." But although one may generally agree that this is true, and I do, this does not necessarily mean it is always true. Might there not be exceptions? If there are, then the rule is only generally true and cannot be bound in every situation.

For instance, if the State were to refuse to formally ratify the marriage of two people who have the God-ordained right to be married, even after intent has been publicly expressed and vows formally taken, many of my brethren would argue that a marriage has not really occurred. In other words, they believe you can't get

---

1 See John M'Clintock and James Strong, *Cyclopedia of Biblical, Theological, and Ecclesiastical Literature*, Volume II, page 544.

married without the State's permission, which indicates that marriage is a privilege to be granted by the State rather than a right to be protected.[2] Such thinking has serious consequences, for if it is true that in such situations a marriage has not occurred, then it seems that it is the State, not God, who has become the final authority on marriage. This, in turn, would mean that the governments of certain Southern and Western states were right when they refused to permit whites to marry blacks, Orientals, East Indians, Mongolians and Malays in years gone by, even though such laws were clearly against the law of nature, against the law of God, and contrary to the spirit of the U. S. Constitution.[3] And if this were to be what one really believes, then I don't see how one could successfully defend himself against the charge of idolatry, in that one who takes such a position would certainly seem to be exalting the State above God Almighty.

Now, one can attempt to deflect such an argument by saying such is a serious charge to make against another Christian, but I fail to see how it is any more serious than calling a brother a "heretic" when he disagrees with one over this particular issue. In other words, when one believes that those whom God has authorized to marry cannot be married because the State, for whatever reason, refuses to formally (read "legally") ratify the marriage, he has exalted the State above God, or so it seems to me, and it ought to be clear by now that the God of all creation does not permit, and will not tolerate, such a view among His people.

---

[2] Refer back to Chapter 2 where the difference between "a right" and "a privilege" is explored in some detail.

[3] It may shock many to learn that anti-miscegenation laws were on the books of sixteen states until June, 12, 1967, when they were overturned by the U.S. Supreme Court in *Loving v. Virginia*.

I realize that those who disagree with me on this do not think of themselves as idolaters, but this doesn't make them any less guilty, and it serves to demonstrate the consequences of being wrong on this issue. The Christian, of all people, must understand that it is not the prerogative of the State to define what marriage is. On the contrary, it is God who defines and authorizes marriage, *and it is the State's duty to uphold what God says.* The State—and I'm talking about any government here (state, local, or federal)—derives its legitimate authority from God. Therefore, when the State, for whatever reason, will not permit two people to marry who God has otherwise authorized, it has overstepped its authority and is demanding obedience to a doctrine devised by demons. This is not just my opinion, but is exactly what the Holy Spirit clearly teaches in 1 Timothy 4:1-2. This means that any government that demands such a thing has forfeited its right to be obeyed concerning that matter. Again, if this is not true, then those who disagree are obligated to demonstrate why. If no credible argument to the contrary can be made, then we ought to be able to agree that God, not man, is the ultimate arbiter of what is and is not a God-ordained, scriptural marriage.[4] With this said, it is time for us to turn our attention to the difference between a God-ordained marriage and the mere legal arrangement the State has dubbed "marriage."

I have frequently heard brethren with whom I'm discussing this subject ask the question, "But isn't it true that a marriage is a

---

[4] It is important to understand that a "right" denotes the freedom to act without asking permission, while privilege indicates a freedom to act, but only after asking for and obtaining permission. Many today, including most Christians, believe it is the legitimate work of the State to grant this privilege. Thus, if the State does not grant it, there is no privilege, according to some. I believe this to be a common but serious mistake. Again, refer back to Chapter 2 for more on this.

marriage is a marriage?," or something very similar. The point they're getting at is the contention that "marriage" is never used accommodatively in the Scriptures. This is emphatically not the case, as I'll demonstrate shortly. But first, it is important to recognize that a legal marriage, that is to say, one ratified by the State, ought to be a marriage that is ordained by God. Unfortunately, history, as well as our current circumstances, makes it clear that this is frequently not the case.

Governments have often appropriated to themselves powers they do not have the right to exercise—*prohibiting* where God authorizes and *permitting* where He forbids. This is surely the case with MDR. The State legally ratifies a multitude of marriages that God has not authorized. This does not mean they are not legal marriages, for they most certainly are. What it means is there are a throng of legally married people today who are not *scripturally* married. The sexual intercourse that takes place in such marriages is, according to God's word, nothing other than adultery.[5] Does the State care what God thinks about this? Unfortunately, it does not! Well, if the State isn't interested in upholding God-ordained marriage, then it has abdicated its authority in such matters. Consequently, the State's ratification of my marriage may be a legal requirement, and I will certainly avail myself of it when it does not violate God's law, but because of the State's lackadaisical attitude about MDR, its legal imprimatur ceases to have any scriptural value, and I believe most brethren should be able to see this.

In point of fact, the State's failure to uphold what God has said about marriage only fuels the confusion over just what, in fact, makes up a God-ordained marriage. A case in point is the charge made by those who hold what is being identified as the "Hailey

---

5   See Matthew 5:32 and 19:9.

position," a charge that argues that the rest of us are actually sinning (by "breaking up" marriages) when we teach that those involved in adulterous marriages must repudiate and repent of such relationships.[6] However, if these brethren did not believe that legal marriages are, in essence, God-ordained marriages, they could not even think of making such an argument.[7]

However, it is not just those who take the Hailey position who are prone to make these kinds of arguments. For example, one very conservative brother told me that if two legally married homosexuals divorced, neither would be permitted to scripturally "remarry." That is, if one of the homosexuals became a Christian, repented of his homosexuality and legally divorced his partner, he would not (as "one divorced for some reason other than fornication") be scripturally permitted to remarry. This confirmed what I had suspected all along, and this is that some otherwise very conservative brethren do not have a clue as to what is, or is not, marriage in our society. Two homosexuals, no matter how many state governments put their imprimaturs on their sinful relationship, are certainly not scripturally married and never will be and, thankfully, in most states they are still not even considered to be legally married. Therefore, when homosexuals dissolve such a relationship, although they will be required to get a "legal divorce," they

---

6   See Olan Hicks' *Divorce, Repentance and the Gospel of Christ* and *Divorce & Remarriage: The Issues Made Clear*, issued as two books in one, 1997.

7   This position is called the "Hailey position" because it was taught by Homer Hailey, a much loved and respected preacher and teacher associated with conservative churches of Christ in the latter half of the 20th-century. Bro. Hailey believed that non-Christians were not amenable to the restrictions Jesus articulated in Matthew 5:32 and 19:9. Because what Jesus said in these verses was part of *only* the New Testament, he argued, *only* Christians were prohibited from divorcing for just any cause.

are not really divorced from a scriptural standpoint, for they were never scripturally married in the first place. Thus, if there were no other factors that would bar them, they would certainly have the right to be scripturally married (one man, one woman, for life), if the occasion should arise.

Now, if I'm right on this, then a legal marriage may not be "a thirty-second cousin" to what the Lord calls marriage. And if God doesn't ratify a marriage, thereby binding the two parties together, then it's not a scriptural marriage (i.e., "a God-ordained marriage"). I think most of my brethren agree that this is true. However, when it comes to the flip side of the same coin, "legal divorce," which may not be any more scriptural than a "legal marriage," they tend to see things quite differently. So, even though they acknowledge a "legal marriage" is nothing more than fornication or adultery if God hasn't bound the couple together, when it comes to "legal divorce," everything changes. All of a sudden, "legal divorce" becomes the deciding factor or standard as to what a divorce really is in God's sight. For example, when a man or woman, or both, put asunder a God-ordained marriage by obtaining a legal, but unscriptural, divorce, many brethren argue that these two people are really (viz., in God's view) divorced. It should be clear to you by now that I don't think so. Yes, it's true that such folks are legally divorced, but they are not scripturally divorced and this, as I see it, is really the crux of the matter.

The Tempest-In-A-Teapot Brouhaha Over Accommodative Language

When two people obtain a legal, but unscriptural, divorce, it is certainly valid to talk about these people as being "divorced," and Jesus used this terminology to refer to such. However, I believe it's not hard to understand that the Lord used such language accommodatively. By this I mean that Jesus was acknowledging that man can, in fact, "put asunder" what God has joined together when obtaining a legal, but completely unscriptural, divorce. Such individuals would be legally "divorced" all right, and God uses this term to describe just such a "putting asunder."[8] However, anyone familiar with what God has said in His word on this subject understands that what He has joined together remains bound together, and this is true regardless of what man thinks or does about it. They know that He continues to hold the two parties in a purely legal, but unscriptural, divorce under the constraints of their covenant before Him. They may be legally divorced, and God acknowledges this, but they are still bound and, therefore, still "husband" and "wife" in God's sight. This is true even when the two parties involved don't know it's true. This is unfortunately and sadly the way it is for many, maybe even most, couples today.

A Total Disregard For What God Has Said

The Bible unmistakably teaches that if two people are scripturally married (and they're not scripturally married unless God has bound them together), then a purely legal, but unscriptural, divorce does not release them from their God-ordained obligations. But according to those state governments that have inflicted upon their citizens the "no-fault" divorce,[9] and this now includes all fifty, both parties of a legal divorce are free of their covenantal

---

8 Incidentally, and most who have examined this issue will recognize its importance to this study, this putting asunder or divorce first takes place in the hearts and minds of those divorcing and is then formalized by the state's legal imprimatur.
9 A concept that has made marriage the easiest of all contracts to break in our culture and is now the law in every state in the Union.

constraints and are, as a result, free to legally "marry" again. All such actions are done with a total disregard for what God has said about it. Now, although God certainly recognizes the unscriptural divorce and remarriage (after all, He's not blind), this does not mean He approves of or authorizes either. On the contrary, He makes it absolutely clear in His Word that neither of the parties in an unscriptural divorce is free to marry again without sin, period. And although it is as unfortunate as it is true that so many people in our culture are totally unaware of this fact, their ignorance does not exempt them from what God has said about it, for it is God, not man, who has the sole right to define and regulate MDR.

Consequently, when a state government ignores what God has said about this, it is, in fact, acting *ultra vires*.[10] I know this is true because the Bible says so.[11] When the apostles said, "We ought to obey God rather than men," they were clearly articulating the principle of "holy disobedience"—the principle that says God, not civil government, has ultimate authority. I am convinced one of the reasons the MDR crisis looms so unpropitiously over the church in our day is because too many Christians have either forgotten or do not know this principle. But before going any further on this, it will be helpful to make a few more observations concerning the Bible's use of accommodative language.

Accommodative Language Is Not Denigrative

The use of accommodative language does not reduce the force of an argument; it actually strengthens it. For instance, in 1 Corinthians 7:10 -11, Paul writes:

---

[10] This is to say, in violation of its delegated authority.
[11] See Acts 4:19; 5:29.

Now to the married I command, yet not I but the Lord: A wife is not to depart from her husband. But even if she does depart, let her remain unmarried or be reconciled to her husband. And a husband is not to divorce his wife.

Notice that Paul is saying a woman who sins by obtaining a perfectly legal but totally unscriptural divorce must remain "unmarried" or be reconciled to "her husband." It ought to be obvious that "unmarried" here is used accommodatively—i.e., this "unmarried" woman, although legally divorced, still had a "husband"—and describes the status of a woman who puts her husband away for some unscriptural reason. She is to remain legally "unmarried" or be reconciled to her husband. If she goes ahead and legally marries, she compounds her situation by adding yet another sin to her iniquitous repertoire (viz., adultery). That this is what this passage says appears irrefutable. Even so, some brethren try to argue it away.

While discussing this passage with a brother who disagrees with me, I was surprised to hear him try to counter my argument on this passage by noting the Greek word translated "husband" in this text is *aner* and means "man," not *husband*. Yes, the word does literally mean "man," but the translators added "her" in front of it to convey how they thought the word was being used in the context. In other words, they believed Paul was trying to say "her man," which in this case would be "her husband." This is also true of the Greek word *gune*, which is used in these verses as well. The word literally means "woman," but the translators interpreted the word as "wife," and to make this point, they added "his" to the word at the conclusion of verse 11, making it read "his wife." How hard is it, then, to understand that by using the term "unmarried," Paul never intended to teach that the wife no longer had a husband? It isn't, and she was, in fact, still scripturally bound to the husband to whom God originally joined her. Therefore, when Paul wrote of the wife as being "unmarried," he had to be referring to the unscriptural, but legal, divorce she sinfully obtained at the expense of her covenantal vows. That the term "unmarried" is used here accommodatively in no way takes away from the truth of these verses. Instead, it enhances it.

In this regard, notice what the Bible says about the marriage of David and Michal. Such illustrates, I think, the force of divine law over and above man-made law. From sinister motives, Saul had given his daughter to be David's wife.[12] While David was later flee-ing from the jealous Saul, the king gave Michal to Paltiel the son of Laish, according to 1 Samuel 25:44. That a "marriage" occurred is clear, as Paltiel was referred to as Michal's "husband." Then David, according to 2 Samuel 3:14-16, sent messengers to Ishbosheth, Saul's son, saying:

> *"Give me my wife Michal, whom I betrothed to myself for a hundred foreskins of the Philistines." And Ishbosheth sent and took her from her husband, from Paltiel the son of Laish. Then her husband went along with her to Bahurim, weeping behind her. So Abner said to him, "Go, return!" And he returned.*

Although Paltiel is referred to as "her [Michal's] husband," she was actually (i.e., scripturally) David's wife. Therefore, Michal's subsequent "marriage" to Paltiel was not a God-ordained, scrip-tural marriage. But that it was, no doubt, a legal marriage is evi-dent, for it had been ordained by none other than the king himself. Can we not see, then, that the terms "marriage," "husband," and "wife" can be used in an accommodative sense, referring to either

---

12 See 1 Samuel 18:20-27; 19:11.

scriptural or unscriptural marriages? *If so, then I believe we can consistently apply what God has had to say about MDR to the various circumstances and situations people get themselves into concerning this subject.*

If God is the one who makes the rules, then His word is the final judge of the matter. Man-made law, in order for it to be valid, must be consistent with what God has said. Therefore, I am convinced that if a husband divorced his wife for some reason other than fornication, he would be legally divorced but not free to scripturally marry, that is, he would need to remain legally "unmarried." But much to the contrary, man-made law would say such a one could be legally married to another. So, although perfectly legal, such a marriage would, according to God's word, be adulterous. This means the man could not marry again without sin. Why? Because God said so, of course, but it can also be seen that although the person's circumstance could legally be called "unmarried," he is still bound to a wife to whom he needs to be reconciled, if at all possible.[13] However, and this is where "the rubber meets the pavement" on this issue (meaning this is precisely where my critics believe I advocate an obvious heretical view), if this "husband" in the aforementioned scenario went out and committed adultery, then I believe the Scriptures, when properly interpreted, teach he could then be scripturally put away (viz., divorced) by his scriptural "wife" for the very cause for which the Lord said one may scripturally put his or her mate away—namely, for fornication. The fact that man-made law, along with some of my brethren, see this as nonsense is beside the point. What I believe is actually the nonsense here is what my critics argue, which is that because she has already been legally divorced and, as they say,

---

13 See 1 Corinthians 7:10-11.

"a divorce is a divorce is a divorce," she could not then, as a legally divorced person, put her "husband" away for fornication. Yes, there is a sense in which a divorce is a divorce, but the question remains: Was it a scriptural divorce? I think even those who disagree with me on this would be compelled to answer "No." Well, if it wasn't a scriptural divorce originally, then the male still has a "wife" and the female still has a "husband." This is not my opinion, but clearly what the Bible teaches in 1 Corinthians 7:10-11. But just so we keep our minds clear on this, it certainly is *not* the case, legally, that the divorced parties are still husband and wife. This is only true in God's sight, and in the sight of those who believe His Word.

The Bible, in Matthew 19:6, makes it clear that man can "put asunder" what God has "joined together." This is done, according to Matthew 19:3, by divorcing "for just any cause." However, the "joining together" is something that God does, not man. Thus, the releasing from this "joining" is something *only* God can do and, in point of fact, the only one God releases from this joining (or bond) is the innocent party who puts a mate away "for fornication." Under God's rules (and the modern State seems to care nothing of this), this person is free to marry again without sin. The Bible nowhere grants the guilty party permission to marry again without sin. In fact, any such "marrying" after being put away for fornication, although perfectly legal and acceptable in man's eyes, is identified in God's word as "adultery."

Consequently, it appears to me that much of the brouhaha generated over accommodative language is nothing much more than—and I hope I'm wrong about this—a debater's dodge used to deflect the heat when the use of accommodative language in the Scriptures can be demonstrated to be a fact. Yes, I think it may be true that some so-called "mental divorcers" engage in semantical gymnastics when arguing their case, but it has been my experience that those who protest the loudest, claiming that the use of accommodative language somehow denigrates Scripture, are actually themselves the most adept at semantical gymnastics. For example, I have never known one of these to use 1 Corinthians 7:10-11 to make their point about the woman actually being "unmarried," that did not either read over the fact that in the condition described in these verses she still had a "husband," or else when they did recognize it, simply tried to explain it away. I said all that to say this: If brethren are going to have meaningful discussions on this subject, both sides must make sure they are not playing debate games and concentrate on trying to scripturally answer their opponent's arguments with honest and reasoned discourse.

In the next chapter, we'll examine an idea that is absolutely essential to understand if one is to make the right interpretation of Scripture as it applies to this subject.

Chapter 8

"Original Intent" And Matthew 5:31-32 & 19:4-9: Who Are The Real "Strict Constructionists"?

When it comes to the interpretation of words, the question of "original intent" is usually in play. I say usually, because postmodernism has changed all this.[1] For the postmodernists, the meaning of words is not to be discovered by determining the intent of those who spoke or wrote them. Instead, meaning is determined by one's own perception of what the words mean. To such people, original intent means nothing. I mention this not because I think those who read here are enamored with such thinking, but to demonstrate there are, in fact, all sorts of ideas afloat about how one determines the meaning of words.

For those of us lamenting the decline of America, we are quite put out with the historical revisionists and judicial activists who are so adept at reading into the founding documents their own political and social ideas. In a rather succinct rebuttal of this kind of thinking, Matthew Bacon, the famous chronicler of English Law,

---

1   Postmodernism is a worldview. It differs from the premodern and modern worldviews, which both agreed that knowledge was certain, objective, and obtainable, and that it exists independently of any personal comprehension of it. In contrast, postmodernism *disbelieves* in objective truth, thinking, in turn, that all truth/morality is relative and situational.

writing during a much earlier time, and specifically about English law, said:

> *A thing may be within the letter of a statute and not within its meaning, and within its meaning though not within its letter. The intention of the lawmaker is the law.*[2]

Commenting on what Bacon said, Raoul Berger wrote, "On traditional cannons of interpretation, the intention of the framers being unmistakably expressed, that intention is as good as written into the text."[3] This has been, and is, the essence of "strict constructionism," whether one is referring to the founding documents of this country or the commandments of God found in the Bible. I'll be expanding on this momentarily, but before doing so, I think it helpful to once again set before you what I said back in Chapter 5 about my basic hermeneutic, which is:

> *I believe it is possible to discover the true meaning of a given text of Scripture by following the rules of grammar and syntax combined with the literary context and style of the passage and the historical, cultural context of the author. I believe there can be only one correct interpretation of a text which faithfully expounds what the author was saying, and this means that all other interpretations are wrong.*

Far from reflecting a postmodern point of view, this hermeneutic believes that God means what He says and says what He means, and that whatever this is is the truth on that particular

---

[2] *A New Abridgment of the Law [of England]*, 8 volumes, 7th edition, 1832, Volume 1, Chapter 9, note 22, cited by Raoul Berger, *Government by Judiciary: The Transformation of the Fourteenth Amendment*, 1977, pages 7-8, note 24.

[3] Berger, page 7.

subject, and this whether one believes it or not. I believe this represents the position of most, if not all, who will read here, even those who disagree with me on MDR. Thus, the question in the mind of the serious student of God's word when dealing with Matthew 5:31-32 and 19:4-9 is: What was the *intent* of Jesus when He said these things? This means, then, that the question is not: Did He say what He meant and mean what He said?, which is a given. Instead, the question really is: What did He actually mean by what He said? Those who disagree with me claim they are the strict constructionists when it comes to these two verses. But in the pages that follow, I intend to demonstrate that these folks may not be quite the strict constructionists they think themselves to be.

The Intent Of The Lawmaker Is The Law

Some years ago, while engaged in a discussion with three bright, well-studied, mature gospel preachers concerning the position I am here defending, I was informed that my mistake was trying to get into the mind of God by trying to discover what He intended to say in Matthew 5:31-32 and 19:4-9, instead of just accepting what He plainly said. I countered by wanting to know why trying to know the mind of God was such a bad idea, particularly when such had to do with trying to understand exactly what He said. Because, they told me, all one can really know about what the Lord intended is by coming to grips with what He plainly said in His word. Yes, I know, I continued, but what specifically was that? Well, they said, He meant what He said and said what He meant. Yes, I know that, I reiterated, but I believe the point is not just what He said, but what He actually meant by what He said. In other words, we ought to be interested not just in the letter of the law, but the spirit as well. Wow, for all the ire I raised by that remark, you would have thought I had said something equivalent to the belief that baptism is really not something that needs to be done in order to obtain the remission of sins.

But Please Don't Misunderstand The Point

Now, please don't misunderstand my point here. I know there are religious people who try to negate the letter of the law, claiming the only thing that is really important is its spirit. But such people are usually talking gobbledygook, as most of them don't even believe in the letter of the law, erroneously thinking, instead, that the "saved" are no longer under law, even to Christ.[4]

Yes, it is true that we are no longer under a system of perfect law-keeping in order to be justified, praise God, but this does not mean we are not under law to Christ. Therefore, I am well aware of the game many are engaged in when they employ that ol' *spirit rather than the letter of the law* dodge. But such a dodge was not my intention then, and it is certainly not my intent now. We are, in fact, amenable to Christ's law, and the letter of that law is extremely important and is to never be ignored, as if it were somehow unimportant. However, and you need to hold on to your hermeneutical hat here, *a thing may very well appear to be a violation of the letter of the law, but not really a violation of that law at all.* Although such a statement makes many brethren extremely nervous, it is an idea, nevertheless, that is clearly taught in God's word. But before actually turning in God's word to those examples where this principle is taught, I think it will be helpful to illustrate this point by something we should all be able to identify with.

---

[4] See Galatians 6:2 and 1 Corinthians 9:21.

A Thing May Violate The Letter Of The Law, But Not Its Intent

Imagine you are walking past a fenced property with a lake when you hear someone yelling for help. Although the property is legally posted with "No Trespassing" signs, you immediately jump the fence and make your way toward the shouts. You soon discover that the yelling is coming from one who is drowning. Thankfully, you are able to rescue that person. When the proper officials arrive, the rescue squad takes the victim to the hospital and the police arrest you for trespassing. Now, what's wrong with this picture? It is, obviously, your arrest for trespassing. But could not a stickler for the law argue that although you did a good thing by saving a fellow human being, nevertheless, you violated the letter of the law by trespassing on property that had been legally posted? In your own defense, you rightly argue that the design of legally posting a parcel of property was never to keep someone from doing precisely what you did. So, even though it could be argued that you broke the letter of the law, you can argue that you never once violated its intent. Anyone interested in justice knows you are not guilty of illegally trespassing.

Now, if one can understand this argument, then one will be able to understand and apply this same principle when interpreting what God has said in His word. Indeed, a thing may very well appear to be a violation of the letter of the law, but not really a violation of that law at all. So, with this in mind, let's see what the Scriptures have to say about this principle.

The Sabbath Law As An Example

In Exodus 20:8-10, the law of God said:

Remember the Sabbath day, to keep it holy. Six days you shall labor and do all your work, but the seventh day is the Sabbath of the Lord your God. In it you shall do no work: you, nor your son, nor your daughter, nor your manservant, nor your maidservant, nor your cattle, nor your stranger who is within your gates.

In defending Himself and his disciples against the Pharisees' charge of violating the Sabbath, an episode that is recorded in Matthew 12:1-8, Jesus said, "Or have you not read in the law that on the Sabbath the priests in the temple profane the Sabbath, and are blameless?" He was referring, no doubt, to Numbers 28:9-10, which says:

And on the Sabbath day two lambs in their first year, without blemish, and two-tenths of an ephah of fine flour as a grain offering, mixed with oil, with its drink offering—this is the burnt offering for every Sabbath, besides the regular burnt offering with its drink offering.

Now, in view of these passages, it is not really all that difficult to believe that according to the letter of the law recorded in Exodus 20:8-10—and please understand that I am not referring to the intent or purpose of the law here, just the letter—the work of the priests on the 7th day would be a clear violation of the Sabbath law (i.e., they would, to use Jesus' term, be profaning it). Factored into this equation is the understanding that any violation of the Sabbath was taken very seriously in that, according to Exodus 35:2, it was punishable by death. Finally, it needs to be understood that capital punishment was not just some idle threat, and this is demonstrated by the fact that the man found gathering sticks on the Sabbath in Numbers 15:32-36 was, in point of fact, stoned to death.

Therefore, it ought to be clear that if one was interested only in the letter of the law, as many of the Jews were, then the priests did, in fact, profane or desecrate the Sabbath by doing the work required of them in the Temple on that day. But the Lord says the priests were "blameless." Thus, we can be sure that the no-work law of the Sabbath was never designed to prevent the priests from doing what God had instructed them to do on that day. The principle of qualification that we dealt with in Chapter 1, when applied properly, informs us of this very fact. Consequently, the serious student of the Bible knows that the intent of a law is just as important as knowing its letter. If this isn't so, then one needs to demonstrate why.

Another case in point is Jesus' healing of the man who had an infirmity of some thirty-eight years. This is recorded in John 5:1-15 and took place in Jerusalem at the pool of Bethesda on the Sabbath. Because they did not at first know who it was who had performed the healing, the Jews confronted the cured man with the charge that he was violating the Sabbath by carrying his bed. This is recorded in verse 10, which says, "It is the Sabbath; it is not lawful for you to carry your bed." In verse 11, the healed man answered the charge by saying, "He who made me well said to me, 'Take up your bed and walk.'" The Jews, of course, wanted to know who it was who had healed him, which they thought to be a violation of the Sabbath, and then who it was who told him to carry his bed, which was yet another violation of the Sabbath, which is the way it looked to those intent on judging only according to the letter of the law. At first, the man didn't know who had healed him, but when Jesus made Himself known to the man, he went immediately to the Jews to tell them it was Jesus who had done so. We are then told in verse 16, "For this reason the Jews persecuted Jesus, and sought to kill Him, because He had done these things on the Sabbath."

This effectively sets up the confrontation that takes place in John 7:10-24. In verse 19b, Jesus asks, "Why do you seek to kill Me?," to which the Jews, in verse 20, replied: "You have a demon. Who is seeking to kill You?" Then in verses 21 thru 24, the Scriptures say:

> *Jesus answered and said to them, "I did one work, and you all marvel. Moses therefore gave you circumcision (not that it is from Moses, but from the fathers), and you circumcise a man on the Sabbath. If a man receives circumcision on the Sabbath, so that the law of Moses should not be broken, are you angry with Me because I made a man completely well on the Sabbath?* **Do not judge according to appearance, but judge with righteous judgment** *[emphasis mine—AT]."*

That Jesus and the man He cured appeared to be in violation of the letter of the Sabbath law, just as the priests working in the Temple on the Sabbath appeared to "profane" it by doing their prescribed work, cannot be denied. But that Jesus and the cured man were actually as blameless as were the Temple priests when it came to the Sabbath should be abundantly clear to those judging righteously, instead of by appearance (i.e., solely by the letter of the law). You may be thinking, well, as far as I know, the cured man may have been guilty of violating the Sabbath. But be careful here, or your Phariseeism may be showing. Note that it was Jesus who had instructed the cured man to take up his bed and walk.[5] Therefore, if the man was violating the Sabbath, then he was doing so at the direction of Jesus, which would make Jesus a sinner for having told him to do so. But if Jesus was a sinner, He could not have been the perfect sacrifice for our sins. Therefore, the healed

---

[5] See John 5:11.

man carrying his bed and the Lord's healing of him—although all this took place on the Sabbath and might appear to someone not judging righteously to be a violation of the letter of the law—were not in any way violating the Sabbath's prohibition against working. The Sabbath, after all, was made for man and not the other way around.[6] This means that you and I can be sure that the Sabbath was never enacted to prohibit man from actively doing good,[7] for against such things there never has been a law.[8]

Answering Hypocrites

According to the account in Matthew 12:1-8, Jesus' disciples were eating, not harvesting. Therefore, they were not violating the Sabbath's prohibition against work, although it is clear the Pharisees wrongly thought so. Furthermore, in Jesus' example of the priests, it is clear that they were doing the work required of them by God on the Sabbath and were, therefore, not violating the Sabbath's prohibition against work when they did so. Even so, in their zeal for what they considered to be the letter of the law, the Pharisees were engaged in condemning the "guiltless." This was a terrible indictment of the Pharisees, particularly when one understands they were really being hypocrites about the whole thing. They had, after all, rightly determined that the work prohibition of the Sabbath was never intended to keep a child from being circumcised on the eight day.[9] They also knew that the priests were not really

---

6 See Mark 2:27.
7 See John 12:12b.
8 See Galatians 5:22-23, keeping in mind that the law was not made for the righteous, but "for the ungodly and for sinners, for the unholy and profane," *et cetera* (1 Timothy 1:9-10).
9 See John 7:23.

"profaning" the Sabbath when they did what God had told them to do on that day.[10] They also knew that pulling their oxen, sheep, or other work animals out of a pit or ditch on the Sabbath was not a sin, although these things, according to Luke 14:1-6 and Matthew 12:9-14, certainly appeared to be a violation of the letter of the law. Is it any wonder, then, that the Lord was so harsh with these folks, calling them "serpents," "vipers," "blind guides" and "hypocrites" who "strain out a gnat and swallow a camel!"[11] They knew what the rules were and had even demonstrated they knew how these rules were qualified; but when it came to making the application of God's law to others, they hypocritically appealed to only the letter of the law, not its spirit or intent. Thus, it certainly behooves us to make sure we are not being modern Pharisees in our interpretation and application of Scripture, and this is certainly no less true when attempting to understand what God has said about MDR.

The Letter And The Spirit

There are two passages that are applicable when dealing with the letter and/or spirit issue. The first, Romans 2:28-29, says:

> *For he is not a Jew who is one outwardly, nor is that circumcision which is outward in the flesh; but he is a Jew who is one inwardly, and circumcision is that of the heart, in the Spirit, and not in the letter; whose praise is not from men but from God.*

(Note: Although the translators of the NKJV and others think "spirit" ought to be capitalized, indicating the Holy Spirit, I find

---

10 See Matthew 12:5.
11 Matthew 23:13-33, especially verse 24.

nothing in the text or the context that compels me to think so.) Commenting on these verses, R. L. Whiteside, in his excellent little commentary on Romans, said:

> *So far as the flesh is concerned, a Jew was a Jew, no matter how he lived; but he was not God's Jew, not such a one as God would recognize, unless he was at heart true to God. Outward circumcision was necessary to the Jew, but outward circumcision was worthless unless it was accompanied by the circumcision of the heart. Circumcision of the heart is the cutting off of the stubbornness and sinful desires of the heart. So many of the Jews depended on outward appearance, but were inwardly full of corruption. In God's sight an honest-hearted Gentile was better than a corrupt Jew. Man looks on the outward appearance, and praises show and display; God looks on the heart, and praises honesty and virtue.*[12]

Physical circumcision was the outward sign of the Jew's covenant relationship with God. It was imperative for the Jewish male to be circumcised. When it was done right, it occurred on the eighth day after birth.[13] The Jews understood its importance and had rightly concluded that the Sabbath law , which came later, was never intended to impinge upon it. Therefore, faithful Jews cut off the foreskins of their male children on the eighth day after they were born, even when that day fell on the Sabbath. There can be no doubt that this outward sign became part and parcel of the pedigree that distinguished any Jew who considered himself faithful to God:

---

[12] *A New Commentary On Paul's Letter To The Saints At Rome*, 6th edition, 1969, pages 65-66.
[13] See Genesis 17:10-14.

If anyone else thinks he may have confidence in the flesh, I more so: circumcised the eighth day, of the stock of Israel, of the tribe of Benjamin, a Hebrew of the Hebrews; concerning the law, a Pharisee; concerning zeal, persecuting the church; concerning the righteousness which is in the law, blameless.[14]

In other words, Paul is saying that when it comes to the letter of the law, he got it right from the very beginning. Now, please keep in mind that Paul was not arguing that he wasn't a sinner, for he definitely was one, only that he had kept the law perfectly, by which I believe we can rightly infer that what he has in mind when he says this is the letter, not the spirit, of the law. Even so, some still find Paul's "blameless" claim hard to believe. But unless one wants to call Paul a liar, I believe the letter of the law is exactly what he meant when he used the term "blameless." But, and here's the point I wish to make, none of this says anything about whether he had ever violated the spirit or intent of the law, for clearly he had, and he admits this in 1 Timothy 1:15, where he says, "This is a faithful saying and worthy of all acceptance, that Christ Jesus came into the world to save sinners, of whom I am chief." Having already said what he had about his blamelessness, his remark here would have to be referring to the spirit/intent of the law, not its letter. This brings us, then, to yet another shocking point: *Something may be within the meaning of the law and not within its letter.*

For example, right after Jesus says, in Matthew 5:20, "For I say to you, that unless your righteousness exceeds the righteousness of the scribes and Pharisees, you will by no means enter the kingdom of heaven," He begins to contrast what most of the Jews thought the law of God said with what it actually meant. When most of the

---

14 Philippians 3:4b-6.

Jews heard, "You shall not murder," they thought that as long as they did not physically murder anyone, they were "blameless," to use Paul's expression. But Jesus makes it clear that such a commandment did more than prohibit physical murder. In fact, Jesus makes it clear that the prohibition went far beyond its letter, piercing to the very heart of the man who harbored ill-will and hatred for his neighbor.[15] And just in case one is having a hard time assimilating this, John succinctly said, "Whoever hates his brother is a murderer, and you know that no murderer has eternal life abiding in him."[16]

Therefore, "...he is not a Jew who is one outwardly, nor is that circumcision which is outward in the flesh; but he is a Jew who is one inwardly, and circumcision that of the heart, in the Spirit, and not in the letter; whose praise is not from men but from God."[17] Could not one rightly conclude, then, that the righteousness Jesus is referring to in Matthew 5:20 is the righteousness that obeys the intent of God's law and not just the letter? And although Paul could argue that he kept the letter of the law perfectly, had he not come to realize that he had violated the spirit or intent of the law? I think it is clear that he did.

Again, Jesus continues along these same lines in Matthew 5:27, where He says: "You heard that it was said to those of old, 'You shall not commit adultery.' But I say to you that whoever looks at a woman to lust for her has already committed adultery with her in his heart."

Adultery in one's heart (viz., "inordinate desire") does not fall within the letter of "You shall not commit adultery." However, the intent of this commandment was to reach down deep within

---

15 See Matthew 5:21-24.
16 1 John 3:15.
17 Romans 2:28-29.

the heart of a man, condemning not just his actions, but his very thoughts. Could it be that Paul, who was no doubt blameless according to the letter of this commandment, might have been guilty of lusting after a woman in his heart? Please don't misunderstand me, for I am not trying to indict Paul with this sin here. I'm just trying to demonstrate that although a Jew could argue like Paul did when making a carnal defense of his faithfulness as a Jew, or like the so-called "rich young ruler" did in Matthew 19:16-22, claiming, "All these things I have kept from my youth," might very well have had a heart condition (and I'm speaking spiritually here) that continued to plague them. In fact, knowing the rich young ruler's problem, "Jesus said to him, 'If you want to be perfect [i.e., correct according to both the letter and the spirit of the law], go sell what you have and give to the poor, and you will have treasure in heaven; and come, follow Me.'"[18] There is nothing in what Jesus says here that indicates this young man had sinned by violating the letter of any law that encroached upon his great possessions. But Jesus knew that the young man, in his heart of hearts, had a problem with such possessions, and this is demonstrated by the fact that the young man was not willing to put the Lord above his possessions. Confronted by Jesus just where he needed to be confronted, the young man who was in every other way a shining example of piety, knew he had failed the heavenly test of his heart and, as a result, "went away sorrowful," according to verse 21.

What does it all mean? At least this: *Without a circumcised heart, nothing else matters*, which is precisely the point Romans 2:28-29 is making. So, although something may not literally be found in the actual words of a statute, this does not mean there aren't principles to be found within the law that, when spiritually

---

[18] Matthew 19:21.

discerned, are more comprehensive than the mere letter of the law. Thus, there can be no misunderstanding that the prohibitions against murder and adultery, when spiritually discerned, address much more than the outward physical acts themselves. When properly understood, such prohibitions address the very thoughts and intents of the heart, the very things that, if not checked, ultimately produce the outward acts.

More Than The Mere Letter

It should be clear, then, that there is much more to God's law than those things found in its mere letter. But saying this in no way belittles the letter of the law, but it does emphasize the fact that one may keep the letter of the law perfectly, but still be a violator of the principles being taught by that law. This is why, according to Romans 7:6, the individual who is truly born again serves the law of Christ[19] "in the newness of the Spirit and not in the oldness of the letter." (Again, although the translators of the NKJV and others capitalize "spirit" here, thinking such refers to the Holy Spirit, I find no convincing evidence that such is the case.)

This brings us, then, to an examination of Matthew 5:31-32 and 19:9. That these passages are absolutely critical to understanding what God says about MDR are obvious. But based on what we've learned about the letter of the law versus the law's intent, it is extremely important for us to make sure we are not interpreting these passages in a way that ignores their intent or spirit.

---

[19] Once again, see Galatians 6:2 and 1 Corinthians 9:21.

Matthew 5:31-32 And 19:4-9

According to the two passages mentioned in the subheading above, the essence of Jesus' teaching on MDR is that if two people are divorced on grounds other than fornication, and if they marry another, they are guilty of adultery. Many have come to think the words of Jesus in these passages are a modification of "the law and the prophets," but let's examine this contention more closely.

Under the Law of Moses, there was legislation permitting divorce:

> *When a man takes a wife and marries her, and it happens that she finds no favor in his eyes because he has found some uncleanness in her, and he writes her a certificate of divorce, puts it in her hand, and sends her out of his house, when she has departed from his house, and goes and becomes another man's wife, if the latter husband detests her and writes her a certificate of divorce, puts it in her hand, and sends her out of his house, or if the latter husband dies who took her as his wife, then her former husband who divorced her must not take her back to be his wife after she has been defiled; for that is an abomination before the LORD, and you shall not bring sin on the land which the LORD your God is giving you as an inheritance.*[20]

It must be understood that this concession of Moses, taking into consideration what Jesus said in Matthew 19:9, was made due to the hardness of their hearts. In other words, Deuteronomy 24:1-4 was not enacted to reflect a change in God's moral intention concerning marriage, which had, from the beginning, involved

---

[20] Deuteronomy 24:1-4.

only one man and one woman for life.[21] Granting a writing of divorcement was enacted to avert a greater evil, for without such legislation a man might unmercifully treat a wife in whom he had found "some uncleanness," even to the point of permanently injuring or killing her. As I pointed out earlier,[22] some say, "but this is absolutely ridiculous, as death was the Law's punishment for adultery." Yes, it was, but where do we find it being enforced by these hard-hearted Jews? Even today, adulterers still deserve death, but there are few courts, and perhaps even fewer Christians, who would favor such a "harsh" punishment. Why? Because of the hardness of their hearts, of course. Many simply do not see adultery, even the kind that takes place in the heart, as the horrendous sin it really is, for many who even call themselves after Christ attempt to justify the harboring of such unholy desires in their hearts as perfectly human and therefore natural. Only when one sees this sin as God sees it will he or she be able to understand there has always been only one reason given by God to sever the divinely ordained relationship of marriage—namely, adultery on the part of one of the partners.

However, (1) because capital punishment required a certain judicial procedure in order to insure justice was being done, and (2) because of the hardness of their hearts no one really pursued such justice, and (3) because the sinned against party in the case of adultery was not permitted to take justice into his own hands, as such was proscribed by God's Law, he was (4) to write her a "certificate of divorce" and "put it in her hand" before sending her away. Therefore, the only grounds God has sanctioned for putting one's mate away is "some uncleanness," which must be, if I've

---

21 See Matthew 19:4-6.
22 See pages 138-139.

interpreted this correctly, adultery. This is why Jesus says that putting one's spouse away for any reason "except sexual immorality" in Matthew 5:32 and 19:9 puts both husband and wife in jeopardy of committing adultery, as both would be committing adultery when they joined themselves to another after being "legally" (in the sight of man) but not "scripturally" (in the sight of God) divorced.

Many Of The Jews Misunderstood Deuteronomy 24:1-4 And, Ironically, So Have Many Christians

The Jews had wrongly interpreted Deuteronomy 24:1-4 to be saying a man could put his spouse away "for just any reason."[23] According to these scribes and Pharisees, a certificate of divorce, no matter what the cause, dissolved not just the marriage relationship but the bond as well, even in the eyes of God. Consequently, they taught that if one secured a legal document, he could put his wife away and marry another whenever he wanted. They were wrong in both assumptions, and the end result was what can only be called "legalized adultery." In fact, and this was mentioned earlier,[24] this was exactly the position of the School of Hillel, which declared it a sufficient ground for divorce if the wife had spoiled her husband's dinner.

So, it is just this kind of thinking Jesus was attempting to correct. (It is noteworthy that when Jehovah spoke of writing Israel a certificate of divorcement [cf. Jeremiah 3:8], it was for the nation's spiritual adultery, not because He was simply displeased with something they had done. And in Matthew 1:19, Joseph was going

---

[23] Matthew 19:3.
[24] See pages 140-141.

to put Mary away for what he thought, at the time, was her apparent adultery.) No, Moses did not permit divorce and remarriage *for just any cause*—the only cause, then and now, is adultery. This is what Jesus clearly teaches in Matthew 5:31-32 and 19:4-9. Hence, it is wrong to interpret these sayings as something new and revolutionary.[25]

With this in mind, let's consider what the prophet Malachi said in Malachi 2:13-16:

> *And this is the second thing you do: You cover the altar of the LORD with tears, with weeping and crying; so He does not regard the offering anymore, nor receive it with goodwill from your hands. Yet you say, "For what reason?" Because the LORD has been witness between you and the wife of your youth, with whom you have dealt treacherously; yet she is your companion and your wife by covenant.... Therefore take heed to your spirit, and let none deal treacherously with the wife of his youth. For the LORD God of Israel says that He hates divorce, for it covers one's garment with violence, says the LORD of hosts. Therefore take heed to your spirit, that you do not deal treacherously.*

Notice that Jehovah's complaint was not that they were adulterers because they had failed to go through the formalities of a divorce. It was the divorcing and remarrying that God hated. Observe further that even though a divorce had been given, and we have to assume this was for every reason other than adultery, the put away woman was still the wife by covenant. Therefore, it is

---

[25] For those interested in a further discussion of this, see "But What About The Sermon On The Mount" in Allan Turner's *The Christian & War*, 2006, pages 59-88.

clear that the prophets taught that "legalized divorce" (viz., divorce "for just any cause") did not morally permit remarriage. So, once again, it is correct to say that Jesus and the prophets are agreed in their interpretation of the divorce concession of Deuteronomy 24. Moses' Law did not grant divorce and remarriage for just any cause, and those who used it that way were guilty of "legalized adultery." Therefore, in Matthew 5:31-32 and 19:4-9, Jesus states clearly God's will as it should have been understood by the Jews.

The Effect Or Purpose Of The Exception Clause

Who, then, was protected by such a law, whether in Deuteronomy 24, Matthew 5, or Matthew 19? It was, of course, the mate who honored the marriage covenant (i.e., the innocent party, if you will). Why, then, should one feel so confident that what Jesus taught in Matthew 5:31-32 and 19:4-9, under certain circumstances, serves to lock the innocent party into a situation that prevents him or her from exercising the very permission to put an adulterous mate away for fornication that is otherwise granted by God in these verses? But this is precisely how those who disagree with me on this subject interpret these passages—an interpretation I argue that may be construed as reflecting the letter of the law while either totally misunderstanding or ignoring its intent or spirit; namely, that God (1) *only* permits divorce for fornication and (2) *only* grants the innocent party the right to divorce an adulterous mate and marry again without sin.

Please realize that by pointing this out I am not trying to dodge what God has said about MDR. Nor is it my desire to loose where God hasn't loosed. Instead, I seek to understand what Jesus taught in these passages, not just on the surface or letter (not that such isn't relevant), but what He really meant (i.e., what was the

intent of His teaching?), which I certainly do not think was to restrict the sinned against party from exercising his or her right to
put an adulterous mate away and marry again without sin, for if it
did, it would turn these very passages on their heads. That this,
along with everything else He touched on in these passages, is the
intent of what He said seems to me to be clear. Therefore, any interpretation of these passages that actually prohibits the very thing
Jesus permitted cannot, in my opinion, be correct. In other words,
no matter how good one's intentions may be, if he interprets these
passages in such a way that actually prohibits the innocent party
from doing what it is that Jesus says he or she has the right to
do—namely, to put an adulterous mate away for fornication and
marry again without sin—then one can be sure he has misinterpreted these passages. Furthermore, the fact that the State has demonstrated itself to be totally disinterested in what the Bible has to
say about this changes nothing, except how the innocent party
wishing to exercise his or her God-given privilege is to proceed,
which is a subject addressed in some length in Chapter 12.

So, Will The Real Strict Constructionists Please Stand Up?!

The pressing question then is this: *When it comes to interpreting Matthew 5:31-32 and 19:4-9, who are the real strict constructionists?* Those who disagree with me think they are. I, on the other
hand, believe I am. Remember, the real strict constructionist takes
into consideration not just the letter of the law, but the "original
intent" of the lawmaker, as well. Thus, an indispensable principle
of strict constructionism says that when the actual intent of the
lawmaker has been unmistakably expressed, it is as good as written
into the law. This means that the cacophony of voices attempting

to speak *ex cathedra*[26] on these passages is not what ultimately defines them. Instead, whatever it is that God actually meant these verses to mean is what they really mean. That is, whatever the words He used in the verses under discussion meant to Him is what these words actually mean, for this, after all, is the very meaning of strict constructionism. Thus, when one interprets a passage in such a way that contradicts something that passage clearly permits, and this regardless of how many charts and diagrams are used to do so, the rest of us can be sure that such an interpretation cannot be right.

With this said, it is time to change gears a bit. Although the next two chapters are rather lengthy, such are necessary, for they address, in a very practical way, the twilight-zone murkiness of the Church-State issues that were introduced in Chapter 7. In these next two chapters, I make it clear that I believe my principal opponents have made subtle, but seriously incorrect, inferences about MDR. Of course, all this has consequences, for if I am wrong about this, then their "heretic" charge is closer to the truth than I have thought. On the other hand, if I am right about this, then it may well be that some of those who disagree with me have received, in a sense, that dreaded "mark of the beast" mentioned in the book of Revelation.

---

[26] This is a Latin term which means "from the chair," which to a Roman Catholic refers to the so-called "Chair of Peter." Thus, when a Pope speaks from the chair (*cathedra*) of authority as the supposed visible head of all Christians, his teaching is infallibly Christ's true teaching.

Chapter 9

The Idolized State

Thomas Hobbes, who was born near Malmesbury, England on April 5, 1588, was greatly influenced by Galileo's mechanistic approach to science. As a materialist of the first order, he believed everything could be explained, and this included man and his politics, in terms of matter and motion. His classic book, *Leviathan*, includes not only two dispassionate sections on Man and the State, but also a highly emotional and scathing attack on the forces of Religion—forces he liked referring to irreverently as "The Kingdom of Darkness."

Hobbes called the commonwealth or State "Leviathan" after the monster described in Job 41. But instead of a creature created by God, the Leviathan of Hobbesian philosophy was a creature that existed as the sole creation of man. Today, Hobbes is generally acknowledged as the founder of modern political theory, although some want to reserve that honor for Niccolò Machiavelli (1469-1527). Even so, one scholar spoke for most when he said, "Hobbes was probably the greatest writer on political philosophy that the English-speaking peoples have produced."[1]

Hobbes' conception of politics was based on his understanding of materialistic psychology. Accordingly, human conduct is a product of human passions, and passions result from a response to motion from external objects. He thought the most dominant

---

1 George H. Sabine, *A History of Political Theory*, 1961, page 457.

passions were fear of violent death and the desire for power, which were in turn mere manifestations of man's most basic impulse, which he called "self-preservation." This, he wrote, was the basic impulse of all men and therefore "a natural right." So broad did he think its application, that he thought it gave men the right to do all things necessary to that preservation, including the right to subdue or destroy others, or to possess their property. However, he recognized that if everyone possesses the right to all things, that it is actually a right that comes to nothing, because total liberty for everyone can only lead to mutual destruction. (Now stay with me on this, folks, for all this is important to understanding the modern State, and how such an understanding relates to the subject being discussed.)

Thus, Hobbes viewed the natural state of man as one of war between every man—a state in which all life is "solitary, poor, nasty, brutish and short." These may be admiral qualities when shopping for a lawyer, but there's not much doubt that these adjectives depict life as a pretty sorry state of affairs.

But, thought Hobbes, the instinct for self-preservation also gives men the inclination for peace. In other words, the desire not to die a violent death or have one's goods misappropriated by another leads the naturally warring factions to seek a lasting peace; and this, according to Hobbes, is where man's reason comes into play. Once man's instinct for self-preservation dictates that peace is the desirable goal, reason immediately suggests "articles of peace." Hence, it is claimed, man's *peace-inclining* passions, supplemented by reason, eventually overcome his *war-inclining* passions. Such is a victory, therefore, not for any one individual, but for the many individuals taken together. In *Monarch Notes: The Philosophy Of Locke And Hobbes* (1965), Sugwon Kang wrote, quite succinctly, the following on pages 12 and 13:

The culmination of the reasoning process, so far as Hobbes' system is concerned, is the social contract. According to Hobbes, the social contract is the foundation of the commonwealth, and, indeed, of all civilization. It comes about when reason directs each man to relinquish his natural right to all things on condition that every other man do the same. Then, since a contract is not a contract unless it can be enforced, reason directs that all parties to the contract agree to set up a sovereign power, with absolute and unconditional authority, to ensure that all parties live up to their part of the contract. The sovereign may be one man or an assembly—Hobbes prefers one man; but it is essential that the sovereign power be unrestricted. The sovereign is the executive, legislative, and judicial power all in one. As legislator and the sole source of law the sovereign determines what is just and unjust, right and wrong, as dictated by the needs of a harmonious social life.

Those who do not voluntarily enter into the social contract, and remain outside of commonwealth, are not bound by the commands of the sovereign, and continue to be in a state of war with one another. This, in fact, according to Hobbes, is the condition in which independent nations find themselves in their relations to one another—in a state of war without benefit of a sovereign power to settle their differences and assure their peace and security.

Reading this, it is not hard to see how Hobbes' philosophy plays into modern-day thinking about Man and the State. In fact, it is just the kind of thinking Hobbes articulated that factors strongly in the security that many believe can only be provided by that "one-world government" United Nations supporters are so intent on touting today. But in direct contrast with the Hobbesian system, the Bible teaches, in Romans 13:4a, that the State was

ordained by God as "a minister...for good." Thus, the only authority the State exercises is the delegated kind, which means the State,
whether it likes it or not, is to exercise its authority "under God."
In direct contrast with what Hobbes claimed, the State has no supreme or absolute authority. Hence, when the State incorrectly
views itself as the supreme authority in everything (or even in anything), it unavoidably begins to think of itself in god-like terms
(viz., as a mortal, although very supreme, god). All such thinking is
idolatry, and the Christian who worships at the altar of a mortal
god—whether it be the State, an organization, or the individual
himself—cannot be pleasing to the Creator and Sustainer of the
Universe.

Enter, Just Here, John Locke

By 1776, which was a significant year for the United States,
John Locke (1632-1704) had effectively refuted Hobbes' theory of
absolute sovereignty. In fact, Locke argued that absolute government is far worse than the original character of nature. Therefore,
he believed that government must remain perpetually accountable
to those it governs. He was able to put forth this argument by as-
serting that the original state of nature was not so hopelessly anar-
chic as Hobbes had thought. On the contrary, Locke believed that
the original state of nature was characterized by "peace, good will,
mutual assistance, and preservation."[2] He believed that all men
were endowed by their Creator with an equal right to "life, liberty,
and property."[3] Not only did Locke's ideas find their way into the
constitutions of many of the American colonies, but they even

---

[2] See Locke's *Second Treatise of Civil Government*, Chapter 3, 1690.
[3] *Ibid.*

found their way into the Declaration of Independence, with some of his unique terminology intact.

Locke's empiricism was qualified, thankfully, by his belief in God. But when others, unfettered by a belief in God, amplified his empirical theories to the nth degree, it fed the secular humanism that seems to have become the unofficial religion of America. Nevertheless, and thanks in part to Locke, the American experiment with representative government did not start out attempting to subvert belief in the Creator and His laws. However, as the now almost thoroughly secularized government of modern America became more and more godless, it started to invoke a god-like status for itself. Consequently, secularized Americans have taken their focus off the God of creation and have replaced Him with the almighty, ever-present State. Christians, as was already mentioned, have not been untouched by this development. Because they imbibed heavily the modern State's arguments for its alleged inherent authority, they now look to the State as the final determiner of what is and is not MDR.

A Prime Example

Every MDR hardliner I know is more than ready to inquire as to whether a particular individual is in a "scriptural marriage" or has been "scripturally divorced." But then, when interpreting Matthew 5:32 and 19:9, they are intent to argue "a divorce is a divorce is a divorce" and "a marriage is a marriage is a marriage." By doing so, they are trying to shore up their claim that the Bible never uses these terms accommodatively. They top this all off with the charge that those who disagree with them are engaged in semantical gymnastics, something they claim that makes it impossible to tell how the Bible is actually using a term in any given context. But as I've already demonstrated, this claim is biblically unsound.

Accommodative language does not diminish the force of an argument. On the contrary, it strengthens it, and the situation described in 1 Corinthians 7:10 and 11, among others, is a prime example of this. In point of fact, it is the ones who argue "a marriage is a marriage is a marriage" and "a divorce is a divorce is a divorce" who are engaged in semantical gymnastics. Why? Because, I think, they have largely bowed to the State as the determiner of what is and is not MDR. In fact, I have actually heard some proclaim, quite unashamedly, that they believe the State to be the "final arbiter" in such matters. Most will deny this, of course, but this does not alter the impact of what they are, in fact, doing.

The Truth Of The Matter

In truth, there are scriptural marriages and legal marriages, *and these are not always the same.* Now, if this isn't so, then one is obligated to demonstrate why. If it is true, then one must accept it and work such truth into his interpretive repertoire. At the same time, there are scriptural divorces and legal divorces, *and these are not always the same.* Again, if this isn't so, one is obligated to offer proof. But if this is true, then one must accept it and work such truth into his methodology. In fact, in their normal queries about one's marital status, hardliners ask questions about these differences all the time. Then, when making their debate arguments, they want to act as if they don't know the difference between a scriptural marriage and one that is simply a legally sanctioned arrangement that the Bible clearly calls adultery. But unless, and until, these brethren are willing to acknowledge that they really do know the difference between marriage as it was ordained by God and the legalized adultery that many modern States call "marriage," I do not see how I'll ever be able to convince them they are wrong on this subject.

Government is ordained of God to protect the life, liberty and property of its citizens, according to Romans 13:1-7 and 1 Peter 2:13-17. Therefore, and consistent with the good order it is required to maintain, not only can it regulate marriage, but I certainly believe it should do so. However, and please make note of this: *This is not the issue we are here addressing.* The issue before us is this: *What are our obligations to a government that flaunts its disregard for what God has said about MDR?* In answering this question, it helps to remember that before no-fault divorce was adopted by most state legislatures (which was eventually completed by the end of the 1970s), the general rule was that a marriage could not be easily set aside. In order to obtain a divorce, it was necessary to provide proof of adultery, abuse, or abandonment. Back then a divorce court judge had the power to deny the request for a divorce if such proof was not forthcoming.

Eventually, and sadly, all fifty states adopted the no-fault model. Under this model, divorce court judges are powerless to deny a request for divorce. All a husband has to say is, "I don't love her as a wife any more," or for a wife to say, "The marriage is irretrievably broken." When such is done, a divorce, according to this law, must be granted. Consequently, an individual's "right" to a divorce "for just any cause" has now usurped all other rights upon which a marriage is based (i.e., rights of children, the other spouse, community, society, government, *et cetera*); and don't forget the ultimate right of God to define and regulate it. All of these have been sacrificed on the altar of individual rights—an altar created by the almighty, self-actualized, autonomous Self which, in turn, is protected by the idolized State. Divorce court judges, with the imprimatur of state legislatures, are but the facilitators of this "exclusive jurisdiction." (Please note that this all bears the footprints of classic idolatry, in that the real power behind idols, other than Satan and his minions, are the ungodly desires and inclinations of the men and women who create them, as is mentioned in Psalm 115:1-8, especially verse 8.)

There can be no doubt that if the modern State still saw itself as amenable to the only true and living God, rather than the whims of its capricious citizens, it would be tenaciously upholding God's law on MDR. Why? Because the truth about this is one of those "self-evident truths" our founding fathers were so fond of talking about: namely, that the integrity of the family (i.e., the Home) serves as the fabric of a vibrant, stable, and productive society. It was, in fact, John Adams who said, in 1778, that "The foundation of national morality must be laid in private families."[4] As W. Bradford Wilcox has written:

> *Adams recognized, as did many of the founders, that the institution of marriage played a vital role in promoting the moral health of the American republic, both by civilizing man and fostering a family environment where children were more likely to grow in virtue. They knew that the new republic's commitment to liberty and limited government depended in no small part on the capacity of American men and women to form and maintain families that fostered fidelity, hard work, self-control, and a measure of independence. They knew, in other words, that self-government begins at home.[5]*

If our government was still the protector of marriage as it was ordained by God, we certainly would not be having the MDR problem we're experiencing in this country—a problem that does

---

[4] L. H. Butterfield *et al.*, editors., *Diary and Autobiography of John Adams*, 1962, page 123.

[5] In a book review of Kay S. Hymowitz's *Marriage and Caste in America: Separate and Unequal Families in a Post-Marital Age*, in *First Things, A Journal of Religion, Culture, and Public Life*, December 2007.

not just affect society, but one that has seriously infected the church of our Lord as well.

"No-Fault Divorce" And Its Un-Godly Effect

I think it is important just here to remind those who disagree with me on this subject that the adoption of no-fault divorce has caused many of them to change their position on MDR over the years. For example, I'm old enough to remember what was being taught on this subject before the no-fault system became the universal law of the land. Back then, most brethren were requiring "for adultery" to be the stated (i.e., written) reason on the divorce decree. If that wasn't on there, then it was generally deemed that a scriptural divorce had not taken place. But no-fault divorce has changed all this.

Although there are still holdouts here and there, most brethren appear ready to accept a no-fault divorce as being scriptural as long as the one doing the putting away knew he or she was doing so "for fornication." If and when the latter can be substantiated satisfactorily, most would agree, I think, that the innocent party may marry again without sin—and this is true, many others would believe, no matter who actually initiates the divorce proceedings. In other words, even if the guilty party beats the innocent to the courthouse, the divorce is still scriptural as long as the innocent party has grounds for putting the other away. But before no-fault divorce, this was simply not the case. Again, there is still disagreement and debate on this among some, but it is clear that, by and large, positions have changed, and they have done so because the State has, over the intervening years, clearly abrogated its God-given responsibility to uphold marriage as the divinely instituted relationship it was created to be. As a result, marriage has become the easiest of all contracts to break in America.

The Mark Of The Beast

Christians who, deep down in their hearts, know it is God who is the final arbiter of what is and is not MDR, have had a hard time adjusting to a government that has abandoned its God-ordained mandate in this matter. Soon, and you can take this to the bank, homosexual marriages will be the law of the land. Short of a complete social revolution, there will be no turning back. This will occur not because the U.S. Congress will legislate such a law, but because the Supreme Court will uphold "gay marriage" laws already established in Massachusetts, Connecticut, Iowa, and Vermont, and which are beginning to appear elsewhere. The argument the Court will make will center around the "equal protection clause" of the fourteenth amendment, mandating that such must be made applicable to homosexuals in every state of the Union. What then? Will most brethren still be arguing that we are obligated to obtain the permission of such governments in order for our marriages to be valid? If so, then it very well may be that all such sanctionings will cause those Christians who receive them to receive the "mark of the beast."

Please don't smirk at this, for some Christians probably smirked at such thinking during the time of the Roman Empire, believing it was necessary for them to burn a little incense to Caesar; after all, they no doubt argued, "Didn't God tell us to obey the laws of the land?" "Besides," they might have declared, "if we don't burn a little incense to Caesar, our fellow citizens will think we are not very good citizens; the government will, in turn, view us as enemies and, by doing so, will withhold membership in the various work guilds, thereby preventing us from supporting our families, and didn't the Lord command us to work so we can support our families?" "Thus," these might have continued, "we are not really bowing to Caesar by doing these things; instead, we are actually faithfully honoring the Lord Jesus Christ."

The Book Of Revelation And Its Application To This Subject

I know such a comparison will be offensive to many. So in order to hone this point down a bit, it is necessary to provide a little background information found in the book of Revelation. Most are familiar with the many warnings sounded in the book. Of the seven churches mentioned in the beginning of the book, only one, the church at Philadelphia, was not given some warning. Although the book pertained specifically to those to whom it had been written, I believe we can learn something from the warnings given to those early churches. For example, if there were certain things the Lord would not tolerate then, we can be sure He will not tolerate the likes of these today. Even though it would be profitable to examine the specific warnings given to these seven churches, such is not something I wish to pursue at the moment. Instead, I want to challenge you to look at the book as a whole. Then, after making some remarks about the general significance of the book, I want to direct your attention to what I believe to be the general warning found in the letter and its application to the subject at hand.

The Overall Message Is One Of Vindication And Victory

Too many people have failed to appreciate the overall significance of the book of Revelation. Its primary message is not one of warning, but of vindication and ultimate victory. In many respects, the book of Revelation is a love story about the watch-care of Jesus Christ over His church and His vindication of it during its persecution by the most powerful political empire on the face of the earth—an empire in league with false religion and receiving its power from Satan himself. It is a glorious and wonderful story. It is one that gives us assurance today as we understand that the Lord will continue to vindicate His people throughout the ages just as He vindicated the early church. Jesus Christ, "the captain of our salvation,"[6] is the Rider on the white horse who slays the enemies of His people with the sword that proceeds out of His mouth.[7] He has vindicated Himself as "King of Kings and Lord of Lords,"[8] and He will vindicate His church as well. The Lord proved Himself victorious over His enemies by making "a public spectacle of them," according to Colossians 2:15, and He continued to vindicate His lordship by successfully defending the church. As He authenticated Himself and His church by destroying both His and its enemies, we can be assured He will continue to authenticate Himself and His church today. Indeed, as Romans 8:37 makes clear, we are "more than conquerors through Him who loved us."

But There Is, Nevertheless, A Warning

Although victory is assured God's people in the book of Revelation, there is also a serious warning to be found there. Those who think a Christian cannot fall from grace find absolutely no consolation in this book, for in it one learns it is, in fact, possible to have his name blotted out of the book of life.[9] And although all things have been provided so that the Christian might be able to overcome his adversaries,[10] such a victory is not automatic. In fact, those who reign with Christ are those who have endured

---

6 Hebrews 2:10 KJV.
7 See Revelation 19:11-21.
8 See Revelation 19:16.
9 See Revelation 3:5.
10 See Revelation 12:10-12.

persecution and not worshipped the beast, neither his image, nor received his mark on their foreheads or in their hands.[11] What I am about to say may shock you, and even more so as I tell you that I believe the book of Revelation has already been fulfilled. Nevertheless, it is my opinion there are Christians today who have allowed themselves to be imprinted with the "mark of the beast" who, all the while, honestly believe themselves to be in a right relationship with Jesus Christ. Let me explain what I mean.

First of all, although I believe the book of Revelation has already been fulfilled, I believe history often repeats or cycles through the same type of events. For example, the church was persecuted by the Roman government and was ultimately vindicated by Christ. Believing, as I do, that the Revelation letter deals specifically with the conflict between Rome and the church, I nonetheless believe that any government in any time can decide to make God's people its enemies and, as a result, bring the Lord's judgment upon it. Consequently, I believe there are Christians today, just like there were Christians during the time of the Roman Empire, who are willing, for one reason or another, to burn a little incense to Caesar. To fully explain what I mean by this, it will first be necessary to consider the Lord's teaching on the separation of Church and State.

In Matthew 22:21, Jesus told His disciples to "Render therefore to Caesar the things that are Caesar's, and to God the things that are God's." These same instructions were repeated by Paul in Titus 3:1 and by Peter in 1 Peter 2:13-14. Historically we know that the Roman government made itself an enemy of the church belonging to Christ. Why was it, then, that the Lord and His apostles taught Christians to be subject to a government that would

---

[11] See Revelation 20:4-6.

eventually seek to destroy them? This is a good question and one worthy of our consideration. In fact, without a proper understanding of the Bible's teaching on the separation of Church and State, one can easily be led into a situation where the "mark of the Beast" will be proudly worn by one identifying him- or herself as a Christian.

Thus, in the following chapter we'll further explore this very important relationship.

Chapter 10

God-Ordained Government And The "Mark Of The Beast"

In Romans 13:1-7, we find a description of civil government as it is ordained by God. It is important to understand the apostle Paul is not saying *every* government is specifically ordained by God, as some have supposed. On the contrary, what he is telling us is precisely what *type* of government (viz., its character) God has ordained. If one understands this, then the difficulties Christians face in reconciling their obedience to God and the State are somewhat mitigated. For example, although many Christians believe that the teaching of the Bible demands they be obedient and supportive of both good and evil governments, no matter what the circumstances, this is not the teaching of Romans 13; nor do I believe it to be the teaching of other scriptures dealing with this subject.

The Bible teaches that the kind of rulers who have been ordained by God are not a "terror to good works, but to evil."[1] They are described as "God's ministers" who have been ordained by Him for the good of those they govern. A part of that good is to "execute wrath on him who practices evil."[2] Christians should be subject to civil government and its authorities not just because the government has the power to inflict punishment for wrongdoing,

---

1   Romans 13:3.
2   Romans 13:4.

but because Christians' consciences, properly instructed by God's Word, tell them that to do otherwise would be a violation of His will. It is quite clear that God has ordained the higher powers and has placed responsibilities both on them and on those to whom they minister. If either the State or the citizens it governs conduct themselves contrary to the obligations and responsibilities God has placed upon them, then both lose their legitimacy in those specific matters.

Justice And Righteousness

Space does not permit me the room to cite the scriptural references, so I'll simply state what all Christians should know—namely, the Bible teaches all governments should be about the God-given tasks of doing Justice and Righteousness. And although many have missed this point, Rome, although a pagan State, administered a system of civil justice that was amazingly equitable for its time.[3] This can be demonstrated from a study of some Biblical examples. For instance, when Jesus was on trial before Pilate, He was tried on a civil charge of fomenting insurrection[4] and was found not guilty.[5] He was put to death not because Roman civil justice demanded it, but because Pilate was a weak and corrupt public official who gave in to the Jews. Roman law and justice "proved" itself in its acquittal of Jesus. But Pontius Pilate "proved" himself by giving in to the Jews' threats, consigning, as a result, one who was totally innocent of the charges to His death.[6]

---

[3] Mosheim, *Institutes of Ecclesiastical History, Ancient and Modern*, Book I, page 2.
[4] See Luke 23:2.
[5] See Matthew 27:24.
[6] See John 19:12.

When Paul was accused before Junuis Gallio Annaeus, the Roman proconsul of Achaia, his judgment was: "If it were a matter of wrongdoing or wicked crimes [i.e., a matter of civil law], O Jews, there would be reason why I should bear with you: But if it is a question of words and names, and your own law, look to it yourselves; for I do not want to be a judge of such matters."[7] This is an admirable and righteous position and is, therefore, worthy of emulation by those who exercise the State's authority. In times past, this was the traditional position of the criminal and civil justice system in the United States. In fact, in 1871, the U.S. Supreme Court declared: "The law knows no heresy, and is committed to the support of no dogma, the establishment of no sect."[8]

When Paul's companions, Gaius and Aristarchus, were accused by an unruly crowd in an unlawful assembly, the town clerk informed the people that if they wanted to assemble to consider some religious matter, it would have to be done in a lawful assembly.[9] If, on the other hand, they had civil or criminal charges against any man, the law and its deputies were available to them.[10]

Again, when Paul was wrongfully charged by the Jews with being "a creator of dissension among all the Jews throughout the world, and a ringleader of the sect of the Nazarenes,"[11] and one "who has even tried to profane the temple,"[12] and would have been killed by the Jews, he was saved by Roman law and justice. Although it is true that Felix, the Judean procurator, was corrupt and held Paul for two years when he should have been released, hoping

---

7   Acts 18:14-15.
8   *Watson v. Jones*, 13 Wall [U.S.] 679.
9   See Acts 19:39.
10 *Ibid.*, v. 38.
11 Acts 24:5.
12 *Ibid.*

"that money would be given him by Paul,"[13] nevertheless, the Jews were unable to kill him due to the protection offered by Roman law. (I am not discounting God's protection, but I am only trying to deal with some of the means He used to protect Paul and others.) When Festus took over as governor from Felix and would have returned Paul to Jerusalem to stand trial, Paul was able to exercise a right provided under Roman law and appealed his case to Caesar.[14] Even though Festus thought Paul to be "mad," he judged him guiltless of any wrongdoing[15] and would have set him free except for the fact he had made his appeal to Caesar, an appeal Festus was under obligation by Roman law to honor.

At the time Jesus gave instructions to His disciples concerning their responsibilities to civil government, we know there was a system of law and order practiced by Rome that, although flawed, was still beneficial to those it governed. And even though Augustus (63 B.C. - A.D. 14) had done much to revive the ancient cults of the Romans, the Jews and, later, the Christians, who were considered to be a sect of the Jews by the Romans, were for the most part exempted from the Imperial cult. Even though it is true that in A.D. 64, after the burning of Rome, the Roman government, under Nero, made the practice of Christianity a criminal offense, it is also true that after Nero's suicide four years later, Christians were given a somewhat lengthy relief from persecution. Therefore, it can be seen that the general domestic tranquility provided by *pax Romana* was beneficial and worthy of support.

In contrast to the God-ordained government of Romans 13, there is the Satan-ordained government of Revelation 13. In the latter instance, it was still the Roman government; but something

---

13 Acts 24:26.
14 See Acts 25:11.
15 See Acts 25:25.

very frightening had taken place. In just a few short years, Rome had gone from a government that offered protection for those doing good and punishment for those doing evil, to a government that protected the criminal and punished the law-abiding. I think it's a good possibility the "mystery of iniquity" mentioned in 2 Thessalonians 2:7 may have had to do with the transition that was already at work, but not yet accomplished, in the Roman government at the time Paul wrote his second letter to the Thessalonians. Nero became emperor of Rome in A.D. 54, the same year Paul is believed to have written 2 Thessalonians. He is alleged to have committed suicide in A.D. 68 and was described by Tertullian, in his *Apology*, as "the first emperor who dyed his sword in Christian blood." Anyone familiar with the terribly perverse life of this man, who murdered his own mother and beat his pregnant wife to death, who had been declared a god by the Roman Senate, and who was the first to bring the unjust wrath of the Roman government against the Christians, would have very little trouble seeing Nero as a part of "the mystery of iniquity."

The Sea Beast

I believe the sea beast of Revelation 13 symbolizes the civil and military powers of the Roman government as these were used by the emperors and other authorities for evil instead of good. God never ordained civil government to be a "terror to good works." Therefore, any government engaged in such activities has, without a doubt, come under the influence of Satan. As a matter of fact, this is exactly the teaching of Revelation 13:2, where it is learned that the sea beast was given his power, his throne, and his great authority by "the dragon." According to verse three, this illegitimate power received a "deadly [i.e., a mortal] wound" that would later be healed. It is my opinion that the suicide of the tyrant Nero represented this "deadly wound." After Nero, the next three emperors (Galba, Otho, and Vitellius), all installed by the Praetorian Guard, came and went in quick fashion. In fact, they were so busy trying to keep from being killed, they had no time to even think about persecuting Christians. There is no record that the next two emperors (Vespasian [A.D. 69-79] and Titus [A.D. 79-81]) ever used their authority to persecute Christians. It was not until late in the reign of Domitian (A.D. 81-96) that Christians were again persecuted by Rome.

It was during Domitian's reign, I think, that the "deadly wound was healed." According to the historian Eusebius, Domitian was Nero's successor as persecutor of the church. About him Eusebius said:

> *Domitian, indeed, having exercised his cruelty against many, and unjustly slain no small number of noble and illustrious men at Rome, and having, without cause, punished vast numbers of honorable men with exile and the confiscation of their property, at length established himself as the successor of Nero, in his hatred and hostility toward God. He was the second that raised a persecution against us, although his father Vespasian had attempted nothing to our prejudice.*[16]

In relation to this, it must not go unnoticed that Tertullian identified Domitian as "a limb [viz., an extension or continuation] of the bloody Nero."[17] Then there is the earth beast of Revelation 13:11. It represents, I think, the perverted religion of the Romans which required citizens of the State to engage in Caesar-worship.

---

[16] *Ecclesiastical History*, Book II, Chapter XVII.
[17] *Apology*, Chapter V.

The Earth Beast

This earth beast is twice referred to as the "false prophet."[18] The Concilia (i.e., the contingent of State priests throughout the Empire) had the responsibility of promoting Caesar-worship and, deriving their authority from the civil and military powers of Rome,[19] forced all citizens to acknowledge Caesar as *dominus et deus*, which means "my Lord and God."[20] That which had been instituted by Augustus (viz., the divinity of the emperor) was fully revived in the tyrant Nero and, after a short reprieve, was resurrected in Domitian.[21] Under such a system, Christians who would not acknowledge the Roman gods, which included the emperor, were referred to, ironically, as "atheists." As such, they continued to be officially persecuted until A.D. 311.

666

Contrary to what many think, "666," although it is definitely referred to as "the number of the beast,"[22] is not really the identifying mark of the beast itself. Instead, 666 is the "number of a man," and is used, I think, to identify those who bow down to the State and its ministers as if they were gods. This could be called Babelism or even Statism (viz., man's effort to deify the State), and all who promote or engage in such activities make themselves enemies of the only True and Living God and are, without repentance, destined for everlasting destruction. The "mark of the beast" appears

---

18 Revelation 16:13 and 19:20.
19 See Revelation 13:12.
20 Herbert Schlossberg, *Idols for Destruction*, 1983, page 185.
21 See Revelation 13:14.
22 Revelation 13:18.

to have been the official certificate or license to engage in the benefits of Roman citizenship. Under such a Satan-ordained system, to
honor the Roman gods and to acknowledge Caesar as divine were
deemed acts essential to good citizenship. All that was usually required of the Christians was for them to buy a little incense from
the Concilia and burn it to Caesar as god. The Roman authorities
made it clear that they did not, in their opinion, have to stop being
a Christian in order to do so. In other words, just burn a little incense today and tomorrow you can continue to worship Christ
was the idea being touted by the State's priests. For many, the
temptation was too great, as burning a pinch of incense made the
difference as to whether or not one was allowed to work in the
trade guilds. No pinch of incense, no job. It was as simple as that.
And, of course, if one had no job then one's family would eventually become destitute. This must have been what some of those
who failed to trust in the Lord thought before they burned their
little pinch of incense to Caesar.

Modern Incense Burners

As I've already made clear, I believe there are Christians today
who are burning a little incense to Caesar in regard to MDR. But
before elaborating on this further, I believe it would be helpful to
view some others who I believe are doing the very same thing for
very different reasons. For example, after participating in a forum
on whether or not a Christian could be involved in carnal warfare,
I was approached by a brother who explained to me rather energet-
ically that he believed a Christian was under obligation to fight in
any war that his government became involved in. This, he exclaimed, was exactly what the Bible taught on the subject in Matthew 22:21, Romans 13:1-7, Titus 3:1 and 1 Peter 2:13-14. Whether
this brother actually knew better and was simply trying to

rationalize his predilections, or whether he was just plain ignorant of God's word, I had no way of knowing. Either will ultimately lead to a rejection of God and participation in conduct that is sinful. But here's my point: *when a Christian says he must always obey the government, then what he is ultimately saying, whether he realizes it or not, is that he will recognize no power above that of the State.* In other words, and although I am sure he would deny it, one like this has accepted the State as his god (i.e., he has received the "mark of the beast").

Although it seems to be a shocker for many Christians, the fact remains that idolatry did not cease to exist with the completion of the New Testament. Babelism/Statism, which is only one of many kinds of idolatry, is very much alive today. This is demonstrated additionally by a school teacher who wrote in one of the popular religious magazines that circulated in the 1980s about the "near panic" she believed prevailed in the minds of some gospel preachers concerning the public schools and the alleged indoctrination of humanism. Although very critical of any criticism of the public schools on this matter, she went on, quite ironically, to accurately identify some of the precise techniques used by the public schools to inculcate humanistic philosophy (viz., role playing, values clarification sessions, situation ethics, *et cetera*). She tried to justify all of this by saying: "The laws of our land, fearing interference with the parents' right to teach their children religious beliefs and/or values, forbids the teaching of moral decisions based on God or the Bible, so the teacher must teach these decisions based on man and his limits and consequences, in relation to other members of society." Her reason for believing it "must" be done this way is—perhaps you've already guessed it—Romans 13:1-7. In other words, this Christian believed that she must teach her students the anti-God, anti-Christian, anti-Biblical philosophies of humanism because this is what the State had commanded her to do; and she, after all, must obey the State because the Bible—that's right, the Bible!—tells her to do so. Here we have, in my opinion, a Christian who had received the "mark of the beast" and didn't seem to know it. She may just have been ignorant of God's word, and this would certainly have been bad enough. However, she may just have been trying to rationalize the type of behavior the State had forced upon her. Personally, I suspect the latter. But here's my point: this school teacher, who was bought with the precious blood of Jesus Christ, did not seem to understand the implications of Acts 4:18-19 and 5:29. These passages clearly teach there are circumstances in which the Christian must disobey civil authorities. In fact, a knowledgeable student of the Bible ought to know that when the authorities command a Christian to do those things that are contrary to the word of God, he or she must be disobedient to those authorities in such matters.

Perhaps you can see that the brother and sister mentioned above are in error. Maybe you even agree with me that they have received the "mark of the beast." But before returning to the MDR question, permit me to further turn your attention to some areas where we could be just as guilty, but not know it.

In Matthew 28:18, Jesus said, "All authority has been given to Me in heaven and on earth." With His all-encompassing authority firmly established in the minds of those to whom He spoke, Jesus instructed them, in verse 19, to "Go, therefore, and make disciples of all nations, baptizing them in the name of the Father and of the Son and of the Holy Spirit." By this, we must necessarily conclude that the gospel is to have free course in the world, and this regardless of the restrictions governments may attempt to place on it. But if we truly believed and practiced this doctrine, then there would, more than likely, be at least a few of us occupying the prisons and gulags of those nations in the world that are openly antagonistic toward Christianity.

When governments tell us we cannot preach the gospel of Jesus Christ within their borders, too many of us obediently obey. When they forbid the importation of Bibles, too many of us dutifully comply. This is all done under the guise of obeying the laws of the land. But what the church really needs today are men and women who are willing to be criminals, when necessary, for the cause of Christ. And make no mistake about it, as soon as we refuse to obey governmental authorities for the sake of Jesus Christ, we will immediately be branded as law-breakers and criminals. But although smuggling Bibles into countries that prohibit the printing or importation of such will be identified as a criminal act, such would not be a sin according to Scripture. In fact, when subjected to such laws, if we are not willing to break them, we are being unfaithful to Christ and His cause. Some, thankfully, understand this and have been willing to disregard such illegitimate laws. However, this concept is made much more difficult within those governments that have not been openly antagonistic toward Christianity. In fact, such a concept is very difficult for most of us. Nevertheless, Western governments, including our own, are becoming increasingly hostile to New Testament Christianity. Consequently, it is time to think seriously about the obligation to engage in holy disobedience even here in the "good 'ol US of A."

One fairly recent example of this country's becoming increasingly hostile to New Testament Christianity can be seen in the 1989 Oklahoma court case involving the Collinsville church of Christ and a withdrawn-from fornicator. In that case, the courts ruled that the Collinsville church broke the law when doing what the Bible clearly says they must do. The church, directed by the elders, was in the process of withdrawing from an accused fornicator when she, in turn, "withdrew" her membership.* The Collinsville church ultimately withdrew from the accused fornicator who, incidentally, did not deny that she had engaged in fornication, only that it was none of the church's business. She sued them for defaming her character in the community and the church lost. As a result, the court directed the Collinsville church to pay the withdrawn-from fornicator $390,000 ($205,000 in actual damages and $185,000 in punitive damages) plus $44,737 in prejudgment interest.[23] (*I know some brethren argue that we can't withdraw from the withdrawn, but most brethren believe the local church can and must withdraw from such in order to remain faithful to the Lord.)

Later, a church in California lost a similar case and was ordered to pay an unconscionable amount of money. As you can imagine, this all had a very chilling effect on churches of Christ's exercise of discipline. Thus, a heretofore minority position held by brethren that taught you can't withdraw from the withdrawn now has court precedent to back it up. Just how many elderships, fearing the results mentioned above, have thought it prudent to just go ahead and burn their little incense to Caesar rather than exercise themselves as the Lord has commanded, I do not know. But that times have changed should now be obvious to us all.

Unfortunately, our government has started to exhibit the telling signs that indicate a transition from a Romans 13 government ordained by God to a Revelation 13 regime under the influence of Satan. But please don't misunderstand me; I do not believe the government of the United States of America is a Revelation 13 type government. But there definitely seems to be a "mystery of iniquity" presently at work in its midst. It is disturbing to me that so many Christians seem to be so oblivious to what is happening in our day. Many associate being a good Christian with being a good American. However, this is simply not true. Yes, it is certainly

---

[23] *Guinn v. Church of Christ of Collinsville,* 775 P.2d 766 (Okla. 1989).

true that, in times past (because of the principle of a government or nation "under God" that this country was founded on), being both a good Christian and a good American were easier than they are today. I am not saying those years were without controversy, for any time a Christian is trying to live consistent with the truths taught in the Bible, there will be difficulties both with society and government. But it can no longer be denied that civil disobedience, long ignored by Christians living in America, will become an increasingly important subject as this country continues to separate itself from the Biblical base that had served it so well throughout the years.

With this said, let's return our attention to the divorce pandemic that currently plagues our society.

Chapter 11

The Divorce Pandemic

One would have to be hiding his head in the sand not to see the Church-State implications inherent in the MDR question. As has already been pointed out, it is God, not man, who ordained marriage.[1] It is God, not man, who authorized divorce for fornication. And it is God, not man, who sets the conditions for one to marry again without sin.[2] When we keep these truths firmly entrenched in our minds, then what the laws of men permit or forbid are not nearly as important as what God permits and forbids. As we've learned, marriage is not a church "sacrament," as the Roman Catholics claim. Nor is it a church "ordinance," as many Protestants believe. The establishment of the church was yet many years in the future when the events of Genesis 2:24 took place.

This means that when two people who have the God-given right to marry are married, regardless of who or what they are religiously, it is God who joins them together.[3] In other words, marriage is a creation mandate and, as such, all men and women are amenable to it. The fact that most of God's creation no longer know this is manifested in the cavalier way many today view marriage. Nevertheless, this does not change reality one iota. When

---

1 See Genesis 2:24.
2 See Deuteronomy 24:1; Matthew 5:32; 19:9.
3 See Matthew 19:6b.

two people who have a God-given right to marry are married, God yokes them together. This means, among other things, that they are no longer considered to be two, but are, instead, "one flesh."[4] Without God's yoking or bonding, there can be no "one flesh" relationship.

Marriage, then, is not something that can be amenable to the think-sos of men. It *is* what it *is* regardless of what men and their laws say it is. When a man and a woman—notice I did not say "a man and a man" or "a woman and a woman"—meet God's requirements for being joined together, He joins them together, period. Two men or two women are not joined together by God, no matter how many states legalize homosexual "unions." Consequently, two men or two women are not now, nor will they ever be, *married* in any real sense. By "married," I mean *scripturally* married. Again, if we (viz. myself and those who disagree with me) can't agree on this, then I don't know how we'll ever be able to eliminate the differences between us on this subject. No matter what the State says, Christians should know that two homosexuals will never be scripturally married. Likewise, they could never be divorced for some reason other than fornication. This means that Christians are wrong when they think that homosexuals, once legally divorced, are prohibited from scripturally marrying, and any such thinking effectively makes the State, not God, the final arbiter of what is and is not MDR. In doing so, one has, in my opinion, received the mark of the beast.

It ought to be clear that the American experiment with no-fault divorce runs aground on the shoals of divine truth. Making MDR primarily a legal matter causes those who do so to receive, in my opinion, the mark of the beast. If it is any consolation,

----

4   Matthew 19:6a.

I believe most Christians who do so, actually do so ignorantly. Most, I think, will be surprised to learn that George Washington married Martha Danbridge Custis without a marriage license. Why then must one have a marriage license today in order to be married? And more importantly, why do brethren think in order for a marriage to be scriptural in the United States today it must be licensed by the State? These are the questions I'll attempt to answer from this point on.

From Whom Does The State Derive Its Power?

This is an important question. If the State derives its authority from God, it will act a certain way; but if from Satan, it will conduct itself quite differently, and this truth is extremely important to the discussion at hand. For example, in the not too distant past, all states in the United States had anti-miscegenation laws. These laws prohibited interracial marriage and were even upheld at the time by the U.S. Supreme Court in *Pace v. Alabama* (1883). Anyone but the rankest bigot will realize these laws were morally reprehensible. By the mid-1800s, some states started to permit interracial marriages so long as those seeking to marry applied for and received a license. In other words, these folks were being given permission to do what otherwise would have been illegal.

This was borne out in *Black's Law Dictionary,* which defined "marriage license" as "A license or permission granted by public authority to persons who intend to intermarry." "Intermarry," was defined as, "Miscegenation; mixed or interracial marriages." However, most of us know what happens when we give the State an inch; that's right, it usually takes that inch and much, much more. Therefore, it wasn't long before some state governments began requiring all those who wanted to get married to obtain a marriage license. Then in 1923, the federal government established the

Uniform Marriage and Marriage License Act. This was later followed by the Uniform Marriage and Divorce Act. Consequently, by 1929 every state in the Union had adopted marriage license laws and "the rest," as they say, "is history."

To make sure we all understand what a marriage license means, it will help to understand the way the state of Ohio, a state in which I resided for several years, describes marriage. In a booklet entitled *The Law & You*, published by the Ohio State Bar Association and the Ohio State Bar Foundation, under the subtitle "Marriage as a Three-Way Contract," those specifically charged with upholding Ohio's laws on marriage do not think God has anything to do with the subject, as they unabashedly proclaim:

> *Marriage is a three-way contract involving the state and the two people who are joined in marriage. The promises made by couples in their marriage vows constitute a binding contract. Under Ohio law, the state is automatically a party to the contract.*[5]

In another brochure they published, entitled *With This Ring I Thee Wed*, which can be found in courthouses across Ohio where people go to obtain a marriage license, they say in the first paragraph, under the subtitle "Marriage Vows," the following:

> *Actually, when you repeat your marriage vows you enter into a legal contract. There are three parties to that contract. 1. You, 2. Your husband or wife, as the case may be; and 3. the State of Ohio.*[6]

---

[5] Visit their website at www.ohiobar.org.
[6] See the website www.hushmoney.org/MarriageLicense-5.htm.

Therefore, God, the original arbiter of what is and is not MDR has been completely and legally expunged from the process. In His place, government now stands supreme, with absolute authority to define and regulate MDR solely as it deems fit.

But Who Gave The State The Right To Arbitrarily Regulate Marriage?

An emphatic "Certainly not God!," is the right answer to the question posed in the above subtitle. Nevertheless, it is argued that marriage is governed by state government today because of the long-held belief that such has a strong public interest in promoting and protecting marriage and families. But with the advent of no-fault divorce, such a claim appears to be nothing but a total fabrication designed to make the State the sole arbiter who defines not only what constitutes a valid legal marriage, but also the obligations and rights that ensue from the marriage contract. Now, if the various state governments involved were the least bit interested in promoting and preserving marriage as it was ordained by God, then their regulation of it would not necessarily be such a bad thing. And furthermore, if the states were enforcing MDR as God has defined it, there would be no need for a book like this, for only those who had a scriptural right to be married would be given permission to marry. At the same time, only those who had the scriptural right to divorce would be given permission to divorce. A government like this would have never authorized "no-fault divorce," which is just another way of permitting "divorce for just any cause." Nevertheless, and I said this toward the beginning of this study, I am in fact sympathetic to what I believe should be the State's legitimate interest in MDR. I agree that government should have a "strong public interest in promoting and protecting marriage and families." However, I do not believe the State has a

God-ordained right to license marriage, as this puts it into the position of supreme arbiter of this divinely ordained relationship. "License," according to *Black's Law Dictionary*, is defined as, "The permission granted by competent authority to do an act which, without such permission, would be illegal." But why should it be illegal to marry without the government's permission? Who gave the government such authority? Again, certainly not God! There is nothing in the Old or New Testaments that gives the State the right to do so. It is, therefore, usurped authority, and as we learned in the first chapter, no one is obligated to obey wrongly seized authority.

Let's look at a few more examples of what's under discussion here. First of all, it may shock American Christians to learn there are governments that require churches to be registered with the State. Although this has not been the case here in America, there are governments that claim if a church has not been legally registered with them, it is an outlawed organization. This means that anyone who is a member of such unregistered "societies," and an unregistered church would be so categorized, is by default a lawbreaker. Within such governments, a locally autonomous, truly non-denominational church of Christ cannot meet the State's criteria for registration, for there will be, as they are quick to point out, no one to hold responsible for any "mischief" due to the non-denominational nature of such a church. Conversely, within the denominational structure of most religious organizations, there is someone (viz., a particular individual or group of individuals who is/are in charge) the State can get its hands on in order to exercise their control over the organization. This means that denominations generally get registered and local, autonomous churches of Christ don't. Here, then, is a clear conflict between Church and State. In this case, one can no longer obey the State and continue to do those things the Lord has prescribed in His

Word, like coming together on the first day of the week to worship the Lord. Even so, I have known Christians who believe that to disobey the State in these circumstances is sinful. But how can it be wrong to do what God says is right?[7] But this is the sad predicament of those who, as was documented in the first chapter of this book, do not understand the nature and limits of delegated authority.

Second, as was mentioned previously, there are governments today that prohibit what they call "Christian proselytizing." Of course, what they call *proselytizing*, we call *evangelizing*. Anti-proselytizing laws make it a criminal offense to preach and teach the gospel in such countries. This means that not only do such governments prohibit gospel preachers from entering their countries, but they make it illegal also to either import or dispense "Christian literature," which would particularly include the Bible, of course. Again, I have known Christians who believe that disobeying such governments regarding these or any laws, for that matter, is sinful. But again, how can it be wrong to do what God says is right?[8]

Daniel's Babylonian Experience As An Example Of What I'm Talking About

Let me say it one more time: *it is high time Christians came to grips with the biblical concept of holy disobedience* that is taught in Acts 4:19 and 5:29. A definitive Old Testament example of this, and there are others, is exhibited in the life and death struggle of Daniel's Babylonian circumstances. Successfully walking the

---

7 See Hebrews 10:25-26.
8 See Matthew 28:18-20.

tightrope of Church-State issues, Daniel faithfully served both his God and the Babylonian empire (viz., its kings and citizens). But in doing so, he did not hesitate to disobey a king when ordered to do things contrary to his faith in and trust of God. What we need today, then is a Church filled with Daniels. Then, and only then, will we be the salt and light we are called upon to be.[9] We are servants of the "Most High" God and it is He "who rules in the kingdom of men, and gives it to whomever He chooses."[10] If Christians fail to understand the implications of this concept, they will fail their Lord and, without repentance, will spend an eternity in a Devil's hell. And unless our government understands this principle, returning to its original concept of God-ordained government, it will ultimately become engaged in wholesale persecution of the Lord's Church. When it does, it will be judged by the Most High God. The consequences will be a nation destined for the pit of God's judgment and consigned to the inglorious dung heap of history.

The continuing role of the church belonging to Christ is presented as one of spiritual warfare.[11] On the other hand, Caesar (i.e., civil government or the State) is given a physical sword (i.e., the penalty of death) to aid in its warfare against evildoers.[12] Unlike Israel of old, the church today is not in the business of taking human life. Such is the prerogative of the State.[13] But in doing so, the State is not free to arbitrarily and capriciously exercise itself, but must do so consistent with the principles of Righteousness and Justice taught in the Bible. The State is, therefore, duty bound to protect the law-abiding and punish the evildoers. If a government

---

9   See Matthew 5:13-16.
10 Daniel 4:25b and 32b.
11 See 2 Corinthians 10:3-5.
12 See Romans 13:4.
13 See Romans 13:1-7.

consistently fails to meet its obligation "under God," and this would be evidence of a Revelation 13 government, then there can be no real Justice. Under such a government, the law-abiding become the prey of not just evildoers, but the government itself. When this happens, society eventually experiences the fiery wrath of the Lord's righteous indignation (i.e., His judgment).

The Christian is to be praying for the State that it will meet its obligation to maintain order in the society.[14] In addition, he will dutifully pay his taxes to support the State, and he will always be found obeying the laws of the land as long as such do not constitute a contravening of God's Word. But, and this is most important, the State has no right to tell the Church what to do in spiritual matters. It cannot (i.e., as it exercises itself "under God") tell the Church when, or when not, to pray; when to preach or not to preach; when to worship or not to worship. In these matters, the Church takes its orders *only* from Christ. Caesar probably won't like it, but he has no power in such matters. In purely expedient secular matters, the Church is obligated to respect and obey the laws of the land. This is, however, as far as it goes. If and when the State seeks to regulate the Church spiritually, the Church is obligated to engage in holy disobedience.[15]

The Church, which is "the pillar and ground of the truth," according to 1 Timothy 3:15, must preach the truth *whenever, wherever,* and *to whomever* it applies—and this application is in fact universal in scope. It must do so without respect of persons. This may involve telling Caesar he is wrong on some moral or spiritual issue. The Truth must always be preached without fear or favor (i.e., not "having men's persons in admiration because of

---

14 See 1 Timothy 2:1-2.
15 See Acts 5:29.

advantage").[16] Yes, the Church is separate from the State. These two God-ordained entities have two very separate roles—one spiritual and the other physical. However, the State is not unaccountable to the Lord's principle of Righteousness and Justice. The State is subject to Christ and will answer to His "rod of iron" if its policies are contrary to His principles, and again this is true whether the State likes it or not. Furthermore, the degree to which a government finds such things offensive is probably a good indicator of just how far down the path toward a Revelation 13 government it has traveled.

If New Testament Christians are not being salt and light, they are sinning, and these sins, if unrepented of, will not only damn their souls, but serve to place yet another nail in the nation's coffin. Remember, "The wicked shall be turned into hell, and all the nations that forget God."[17]

Because civil government (and this refers to the *concept* of civil government and not the particular *form* such government might take) has been ordained by God, its every ordinance is to be obeyed. Necessarily, then, the "every ordinance of man" mentioned in 1 Peter 2:13 *cannot* include those things God has not authorized or otherwise prohibited. As was previously mentioned, such qualify the "every ordinance" man is required to obey. Therefore, the State has a place in the scheme of things and, as such, should have, or at least it seems so to me, a vested interest in MDR. Nevertheless, I can find nothing in the Scriptures that indicate the State ought to be in the business of licensing marriage. Instead, its task, as I see it, is to *recognize* God-ordained marriages, *regulate* divorce for only the God-ordained reason, and *prosecute* any crimes

---

16 Jude 16.
17 Psalm 9:17.

associated with either of these when committed (e.g., adultery, big-amy, *et cetera*). Of course, the modern State has taken upon itself the right to license marriage. At the same time, it permits divorce for just any cause and no longer prosecutes for adultery. What a sad state of affairs, no pun intended.

The Unchecked State Is A Political Idol

When the State leaves God's standard of authority, it is inevitable that it will arbitrarily and capriciously enforce its own rules and regulations. For example, in the fair state of Mississippi, where I recently lived, a blood test is still required in order to obtain a marriage license. If it is discovered that one of the parties has a venereal disease, then the state government will not permit the marriage to take place until the offending party is disease free. However, if it is discovered that one of the parties has AIDS, this will not only *not* be made public, it will not prohibit the marriage. Go figure!

The times in which we live are quite evil. The condemnation of the ancient prophet rings true in our land today: "Justice is turned back, and righteousness stands afar off: for truth is fallen in the street, and equity cannot enter. So truth fails, and he who departs from evil makes himself a prey."[18] Americans today are standing at a crossroads. Secularism, Humanism, and Statism (i.e., the 666 syndrome), if allowed to continue unchecked, will eventually make of us either converts to this unholy trinity or criminals of the State. It is my prayer that all who wear the name of the glorious Christ will have the backbone of faith, with God's help, to withstand the onslaught of the beast.

---

[18] Isaiah 59:14-15.

So, as I see it, the State has not been authorized by God to license marriage and those who think it is are either statists or duped. Either category manifests the mark of the beast. Gospel preachers and Christians who teach that in order for a marriage to be scriptural it must be licensed by the State are sorely mistaken. They have fallen for that old line of the Concilia so many years ago: "Burning a little incense to Caesar [they would, of course, never describe it this way] doesn't keep you from being a good Christian, it just means you're being a good citizen of the realm." "But keep this in mind," the Concilia would have menacingly added, "if you refuse to purchase some incense and publicly burn it to Caesar, we'll make your life, and maybe even your death, as miserable as possible."

Unfortunately, many today have the mistaken idea that the moral standard contained in the Bible is limited to a certain group of people: namely, Christians. I'm afraid this idea is even being imbibed by more and more Christians. Making this mistake, secularists believe Biblical ethics have no place in the public square. They argue that Christians must keep their code of ethics (i.e., the standard of Justice and Righteousness taught in the Bible) under wraps, confining these within the walls of their homes and church-buildings. These advocates of the "naked public square" (i.e., a completely secularized society) view folks like me with a jaundiced eye. Anyone, they think, who advocates imposing a code of ethics across an entire society—and I believe every right-thinking Christian is certainly guilty of this—is not just intolerant and bigoted, but dangerous as well. When this sentiment finally becomes enacted into law, faithful Christians (i.e., those who have not received the mark of the beast) will be persecuted, imprisoned, and eventually executed. I do not think this is about to happen, but the stew of such a sentiment is already being stirred in our culture. Without national repentance, I am convinced that this can, and will, happen. Therefore, the interaction of Church and State (i.e., the sacred and secular) is extremely important to individual Christians, as well as the whole nation.

That this exact sentiment was expressed in the "original intent" of the Founding Fathers of the American republic is well attested to. In his excellent book, *Faith & Freedom: The Christian Roots Of American Liberty*, Benjamin Hart wrote, "Even if one does not accept the truth of the Christian faith, prudence argues for the promulgation of its moral code in every area of public life, because history has demonstrated that Christian morality is indispensable to the preservation of a free society."[19] This agrees with what the Frenchman Alexis de Tocqueville reported in his early 19th century *Democracy in America*, a classic of political and sociological reporting, in which he wrote, America is "the place where the Christian religion has kept the greatest power over men's souls; and nothing better demonstrates how useful and natural it is to man, since the country where it now has the widest sway is both the most enlightened and the freest." Commenting further on the truth of this, Hart wrote:

> *In his essay "What I Saw in America," the great English writer G. K. Chesterton observed that "America is the only nation in the world that is founded on a creed. That creed is set forth with dogmatic and even theological lucidity in the Declaration of Independence." Chesterton was referring to the second paragraph of America's founding document which states: "We hold these truths to be self-evident, that all men are created equal, that they are endowed by their Creator with certain unalienable rights, that among these are life,*

---

[19] 1988, page 15.

liberty and the pursuit of happiness" (emphasis added). The starting point of the Declaration's argument was faith in man's "Creator," and is very similar to the Apostle Paul's initial proposition in his letter to the Romans: "Because that which is known about God is evident within them; for God made it evident to them. For since the creation of the world His invisible attributes, His eternal power and divine nature, have been clearly seen, being understood through what has been made, so that they are without excuse" (Romans 1:19-20).

Toward the end of his book, Hart summarized by saying:

> *This is important [he's speaking here specifically of the application of religious principles to political science] , because the design of a political order at root is a religious issue, contingent on certain assumptions about the origin and nature of man; the kind of God to whom we will be held accountable; how we order our values; our conception of rights and obligations; and how we are to treat our neighbors either in person or through the instrument of the state. Certainly religion is a personal matter; but it has deep social and political implications. Every social order rests on certain religious assumptions, sometimes explicitly and sometimes implicitly.*[20]

We were fortunate that the American Republic was created in a time when there was so much unanimity about what constituted good government. Unfortunately, our post-Christian culture has clearly lost its way. Nevertheless, and most ironically, this same culture can frequently be heard clamoring for justice and the doing

---

[20] Hart, pages 337-338.

of what is right. But, our post-Christian and now post-modern culture has summarily rejected that absolute standard of Righteousness taught in the Bible, a standard that is absolutely necessary if real acts of Justice are to be consistently carried out. ("Post-modernism" is a term that happens to be in vogue right now. Therefore, I use it here for reference purposes; but it must be understood that post-modernism represents nothing much more than the collective and effete think-sos of our post-Christian culture.) Consequently, as our nation continues down paganism's slippery slope, everything that was once thought to be morally right will be questioned and ultimately rejected. Without national repentance, divine judgment will eventually result.[21] Make no mistake about it, the Bible makes it clear that God's adversaries, when the time is right,[22] will meet the fire of His wrath. Why? Because, as has already been pointed out, they have seen fit to neglect God's absolute standard of Righteousness,[23] and "Righteousness," the Bible tells us, "exalts a nation; but sin is a reproach to any people."[24]

Interesting Irony

Thus, I find it ironic that those who boldly argue that "a marriage is a marriage is a marriage" and "a divorce is a divorce is a divorce," which are just arguments for defending the State's alleged authority to define MDR, and who are themselves people who I think just may have received the "mark of the beast," blindly see themselves in a position to call me a "heretic" for arguing it is *only* God who has the authority to rightfully regulate MDR. They will

---

21 See Isaiah 13-23; Jeremiah 46-51; Ezekiel 25-32; Amos 1-2, *et cetera*.
22 See Genesis 15:16.
23 See Psalm 97:1-9.
24 Proverbs 14:34.

say this is not true, of course, so I am interested it what they will offer in their defense.

I have told my Christian friends who disagree with me on this subject that I would love to find out I'm wrong, for then I could feel comfortable within *the walls of church-of-Christ orthodoxy*. For those of you who are offended by my terminology, I'm sorry, but I don't know how else to describe what I'm talking about here and, after all, it is what it is. Again, I don't like being in the minority on this—a minority that is readily identified by those who are "orthodox" as false teachers, heretics, and spiritual scalawags. So yes, such makes me uncomfortable. Nevertheless, I remain convinced that to preach or teach any other position than the one I am here defending would be a failure to "contend earnestly for the faith which was once for all delivered to the saints."[25]

The fact that my belief on this has prevented, and more than likely will continue to prevent, me from serving the Lord in a capacity I have spent most of my adult life preparing for, namely, serving as an elder, is but part of the price I have paid. I'm not saying this to generate sympathy, for such simply goes with the territory, and as my mother would no doubt remind me, "Son, you're a big boy now, so take it like a man." But I make reference to this in order to make it clear that I understand the position I am here defending has personal consequences. But if such were to keep me from preaching and teaching what I believe to be the truth on this subject, then I would not be faithful, at least from my point of view, to Him who bought me with His own blood, and as Revelation 21:8 makes graphically clear, "The cowardly...shall have their part in the lake which burns with fire and brimstone, which is the second death."

---

[25] Jude 3.

Chapter 12

What Are Christians To Do?

Although what I've said up to this point may cause some of you to think otherwise, nothing I've written here should be construed to mean I think it is inherently wrong for a Christian to go through the marriage license procedure in order to obtain an official certificate that provides legal proof that he or she is married. I don't. Although I admit to being uncomfortable with the "license" concept, I view the marriage certificate that results from the process to be a public ratification of the God-ordained relationship of marriage. Notice what I said about this previously:

> [I]t appears reasonable that there are, ideally, three things required for a scriptural, God-ordained marriage to occur: (1) a statement of intent, (2) an oath (or vow) by each to observe the terms of the covenant, and (3) some form of ratification of the covenant by a public, culturally accepted act, usually coincident with the oath itself.[1]

Therefore, I do not have to agree with the State's thinking it has the right to license marriage in order to comply with the requirement, as such serves to make public the marriage contract entered into by the two parties involved. However, if the State were to refuse a marriage license to those who are scripturally authorized to

---

[1] Page 146.

marry, I would not see this as a legitimate impediment to the solemnization and ratification of such a marriage. What I mean by the use of "legitimate impediment" is this: The State, which has been ordained by God with delegated authority, does not have the legitimate power to prevent two people who have the God-given right to be married from being married, and where there is no legitimate authority, one is not obligated to obey.

But how, you might ask, could this be done? The Scriptures say, in 1 Peter 4a, that "If anyone speaks, let him speak as the oracles of God." Therefore, I direct you to 1 Corinthians 6:1-11, which I think offers just such a model.

> *Dare any of you, having a matter against another, go to law before the unrighteousness, and not before the saints? Do you not know that the saints will judge the world? And if the world will be judged by you, are you unworthy to judge the smallest matters? Do you not know that we shall judge angels? How much more, things that pertain to this life? If then you have judgments concerning things pertaining to this life, do you appoint those who are least esteemed by the church to judge? I say this to your shame. Is it so, that there is not a wise man among you, not even one, who will be able to judge between his brethren? But brother goes to law against brother, and that before unbelievers! Now therefore, it is already an utter failure for you that you go to law against one another. Why do you not rather accept wrong? Why do you not rather let yourselves be defrauded? No, you yourselves do wrong and defraud, and you do these things to your brethren! Do you not know that the unrighteous will not inherit the kingdom of God? Do not be deceived. Neither fornicators, nor idolaters, nor adulterers, nor homosexuals, nor sodomites, nor thieves, nor covetous, nor drunkards, nor revilers, nor extortioners*

will inherit the kingdom of God. And such were some of you. But you were washed, but you were sanctified, but you were justified in the name of the Lord Jesus and by the spirit of our God.

Although 1 Corinthians 6:1-11 is specifically speaking of a Christian "having a matter against another" and thus going "to law before the unrighteous, and not before the saints," I believe there is a principle here that can be applied to matters involving MDR, at least in some aspects, and particularly when the State has disregarded its God-given authority by attempting to speak where God has not given it permission to speak. Although this passage does not negate the God-ordained function of civil government set forth in Romans 13, 1 Pet. 2, and other places, it does speak to the unrighteous bent all too prevalent in pagan courts of law. Unfortunately, our present court system is becoming more and more pagan. Sadly, the Most High God has been effectively expunged from its rulings. The shrill cry of the "separation of Church and State" has been used by the secularists to denude all of government and much of society regarding the moral and ethical influences of faith in the Creator. Consequently, whatever positive influence the State once exercised over MDR has been completely erased in our times. It is time, therefore, that Christians learned to depend upon the judgments of their fellow Christians regarding many things, including MDR.

Therefore, if the State, as it once did, and still does in some cases, refused to license a marriage between two people who have a God-given right to marry, this ought not to be an insurmountable problem for Christians, for they have a ready-made community before whom they can solemnize and formalize their marriages. (For the sake of those who believe marriage ceremonies ought not to be conducted in the church's meeting-house because they are, in their opinion, a purely civil matter that has nothing to do with the work of the local church, it would not be necessary for the marriage ceremony to be conducted in the meeting house in order to be official. On the other hand, in light of what has been discussed in this book, it might be time to rethink such a position.) Such a marriage would not be legal according to the pagan or neo-pagan State, but the two being joined in God-ordained matrimony would have the assurance of knowing they were married in the sight of God and the eyes of that one community that remains in a position to know what true God-ordained marriage really is—namely, the church of Jesus Christ.

But without the State's permission and legal ratification, some among us are contending that such a marriage would be nothing but a sham (i.e., not a real marriage at all). I believe such thinking is wrong, and if you disagree with me on this, could it be because you have acquiesced in burning a little incense to Caesar?

Again, where in God's word is there authorization for the State to prohibit those with a scriptural right to marry from marrying? There is, in fact, none; and any such doctrine must be understood to be spawned by demons.[2] This means that gospel preachers who teach a marriage isn't a marriage until and unless the State says so are just plain wrong. They are not speaking, in other words, as "the oracles of God."[3]

Some will no doubt want to countercharge by accusing me of believing in something they may wind up calling "mental marriage." But just like the charge of "mental divorce," I don't think I'm guilty. Nonetheless, if by "mental marriage" they mean to identify the scenario articulated above, then I suppose I ought to

---

2   See 1 Tim. 4:1-5.
3   1 Peter 4:11.

just plead guilty. But guilty of what: violating God's word or the think-sos of men? Only the latter, in my humble opinion.

This brings us once again, then, to the question of so-called "mental divorce." I no more believe in and promote "mental divorce" than I do "mental marriage." But for the sake of defending the position some have characterized as "mental divorce," I pled guilty at the beginning of this study. It has been my experience that the Mental Divorce moniker conjures up all sorts of ideas about what I and others believe and, as I've already stated, I think it is an unjustly prejudicial appellation—an appellation that distorts the subject being discussed. Thus, it ought to be dropped. But I rather doubt it will be. Even so, and with 1 Corinthians 6:1-11 in mind, I would like for you to consider a scenario having to do with the subject of divorce and how the saints could be involved. The fact that such a remedy is not practiced among churches of Christ today does not mean that it could not be. What's more, the fact that the process I'll be talking about is not being practiced among any of the churches of Christ that I am aware of bolsters, rather ironically I think, the so-called Mental Divorce charge that has been unfairly and too casually bantered about. Permit me to explain by means of the following hypothetical situation.

Hypothetical Circumstances And A Proposed Process

Let's say, God forbid, that my beautiful wife of 43 years decides to divorce me for some reason other than fornication. Even though I have tried to talk her out of it, seeking the advice of the elders and/or other members of the local church of which I am a member, she decides to divorce me anyway. Is there anything, short of me murdering her, that could prevent her from doing so? No, not under the present no-fault system.

Continuing to describe the facts of this hypothetical scenario, as far as I can ascertain, she has not committed adultery. Consequently, I know that if divorced by her in this way, I must remain celibate or else be guilty of adultery. She divorces me. I remain celibate. I still love her and know we are still bound by God. In other words, I understand that biblically she is still my "wife" and I am still her "husband."[4]

I try to reconcile, continuing to ask the local church to assist me in this effort. All such attempts fail. Afterward—and I do not, as some do, see the amount of time elapsing before the next event to be significant—she marries another. Because she is still scripturally my wife, and because she is now engaged in adultery, I believe I have the God-given right to put her away "for fornication,"[5] which I understand to be the *only reason* God has given for divorcing and marrying again without sin. But because my wife and I are now in the post-legal divorce stage, many of my fellow Christians think the unscriptural divorce granted by a government that has clearly overstepped its God-ordained bounds prevents me from exercising the right the Lord gave me to put my fornicating mate away. Remember, please, that a God-given right cannot be interfered with by the State or anyone else. How is it, then, that the ungodly actions on the part of my wife and the State stand in the way of me exercising my God-given right? Can God and His law be so easily defeated? Am I to obey God or man in this matter? Yes, I know man can and does violate God's law. I realize we live in a sinful world. However, the principles taught in God's word remain true no matter what man thinks or does.

---

4   1 Corinthians 7:10-11.
5   Matthew 19:9.

Fortunately (remember, this is only a hypothetical), the local church I am a member of believes my wife, by committing adultery, may now be scripturally put away by me. Nonetheless, the State, which cares nothing about such matters, already considers us to be divorced. It is, therefore, not the least bit interested in my claim about a scriptural right to put my wife away "for fornication." What, then, am I to do? Those who take a position different than my own argue that the *only* avenue open to me at this point would be to put my wife away mentally (i.e., just in my own mind), and this, they say, is totally unscriptural.

Let me first counter by saying I do not know of any marriage or divorce that does not begin in the mind. So yes, the repudiation of my wife because of her fornication is something I must mentally decide to do. But if this is what makes a post-legal divorce a "mental divorce," and therefore wrong, then I fail to see how *any* divorce could escape this charge. Thus, it cannot be true that the repudiation of my wife for fornication, which is something that must *first* take place in my own mind, is what makes some claim that such is just a "mental divorce" and therefore unscriptural. There must be some other reason, and there is.

The reason the action I am here defending is called "mental divorce" is because those who use this terminology believe the State, because it is the State, has the sole authority to grant a divorce for just any cause.[6] Thus, it is claimed, when the State exercises itself and grants a divorce for any reason except fornication, the innocent party, who is so divorced, no longer has any God-given right to put his or her mate away, as it is the State's imprimatur, and this alone, that defines and delineates divorce. But such thinking is totally without any scriptural merit. The State, which is only per-

---

6   It did in the first century and it does so now.

mitted to exercise delegated authority, has been given absolutely no authority by God to grant divorce for just any cause. Wrongly thinking it has been, many think the innocent party (i.e., the only one who God granted permission to put away a mate for fornication and marry again without sin) is forever locked into a situation that prevents him or her from doing the very thing the Lord granted permission to do—namely, to repudiate a fornicating mate and, if one chooses, marry again without sin. But can this really be true? Is God's law to be so easily trumped by the State? More to the point, can the State's law actually supercede God's law? If it can, then the State, not God, has become the final arbiter of what is and is not divorce. This makes the State, in the minds of such people, not just *a god*, but *the God*. They can protest all they want, but this is the logical result of such thinking, and if such thinking isn't deserving of being identified with the mark of the beast, then I am at a loss to understand anything.

Yes, the State can, and often does, arbitrarily define divorce completely contrary to what God has said in His word. The Bible calls this "putting asunder what God has joined together." But when it does so, the innocent party is not without recourse, or at least they shouldn't be, for there is usually no more qualified group of people for deciding what is or is not a scriptural divorce than those who make up the local church. I hedge this statement with what the apostle Paul said in 1 Corinthians 6:2:

> *Do you not know that the saints will judge the world? And if the world will be judged by you, are you unworthy to judge the smallest matters?*

But because it can be effectively argued (and I think correctly so) that the State has a God-ordained interest in MDR, and this because of MDR's affect on the stability of society, I would (and I'm speaking now of the hypothetical scenario under consideration), if granted the opportunity, seek remedy in the civil divorce court. Sadly, of course, the State will not only think my suit to be just foolishness, but deem it to be without any standing at law. But such law would be the State's law, not God's. Consequently, I will take my case to the local church—an interested community who will diligently examine my claim and then judiciously decide whether I do or do not, in fact, have the right to scripturally put my wife away "for fornication." (Remember that in this hypothetical situation I am a member of a local congregation that is attuned to my plight and believes the principles taught by the apostle Paul in 1 Corinthians 6:1-11 are still applicable.)

The fact that my wife is now legally married to another man will be my strongest evidence that she is committing fornication and that I, therefore, have the scriptural right to put her away for this cause. However, this evidence alone, although compelling, would not be sufficient for my local church to decide in my favor. Stay with me on this and you'll see what I'm talking about.

Commensurate with the obligations God's Word has placed upon a husband toward his wife, the church will want to establish to the best of its ability that I am not guilty of any wrongdoing in the matter at all. For example, the husband is to love his wife just as Christ loved the church. If it could be substantiated that I had not done this, such would be sufficient reason for the church to deny my petition. Further, as 1 Peter 3:7 points out, a husband is instructed to live with his wife "with understanding, giving honor to the wife, as the weaker vessel, and as being heirs together of this grace of life, that your prayers may not be hindered." The phrase "that your prayers may not be hindered" indicates that God places a tremendous responsibility on the wife's husband. He is, according to Ephesians 5:23, the head of his wife and, as such, it is his responsibility to dwell with her "with understanding, as the weaker vessel." And just what is this "knowledge," as the KJV renders it? I like very much what R.C.H. Lenski says about it:

> *The wife is the weaker vessel. Paganism always tends to abuse her on this account. Her rights are reduced, often greatly. Her status is lowered, often shamefully. Heavy loads are put upon her. She is made man's plaything or man's slave. The fact that she is weaker is always exploited. That is why Peter inserts the phrase regarding "knowledge." Christian knowledge will accord the wife all the consideration and the thoughtfulness which God intends for her "as a weaker vessel" in her "wifely" relation.*[7]

He goes on to say:

> *While she is "a weaker vessel," every Christian wife is "also" an heir of God's grace, and there is no difference in this respect between her and her Christian husband (Gal. 3:28).*[8]

Therefore, if it could be demonstrated that I had not done this, such would be sufficient grounds to reject my petition, for a Christian husband who could not expect God to hear his prayers—and this because he persists in, or falls back into, the old pagan ignorance in the treatment of his wife—could not hope to be thought of as a purely innocent party with the right to put his mate away for fornication.

And there is more, for if it could be demonstrated that I had failed to render to my wife "the affection due her" that 1 Corinthians 7:3 commands, then it could not be fairly decided that I was, in

---

[7] Lenski, *The Interpretation Of 1 And 2 Epistles Of Peter, The Three Epistles Of John, And The Epistles Of Jude*, 1966, p. 139.
[8] *Ibid.*

fact, an innocent party in the matter. Consequently, the church could neither agree with nor ratify my decision to put my wife away, as my actions could be deemed as having caused her to commit adultery or, in some way, contributing to it.[9]

On the other hand, if the church found in my favor, then they would "permit," "ratify," or whatever else you might want to call it, my right to put my wife away. They would, more than likely, decide to record their findings as a part of the permanent record. Any other congregation with a legitimate interest in my status could enquire and be informed of the findings. This, of course, would not mean that the interested congregation would be required to accept the findings of the ratifying congregation, but such ought to give credence to the fact that I had not tried to personally rectify the State's usurpation and subsequent indifference by simply *mentally divorcing* my wife. On the contrary, and continuing to remember that this is merely a hypothetical situation, no effort was made to keep private a totally public decision to repudiate a fornicating mate consistent with the teaching of God's Word. Although such a procedure would not, at the moment, be considered legal, it would, or so it seems to me, be right and honorable in the sight of God and His people.

Such A Process Has Value In A Pre-Legal Divorce As Well

Now, because the Scriptures direct us to submit to civil government when and where possible (and I realize we are walking a spiritual and legal tightrope here), I believe a Christian who is scripturally justified in obtaining a divorce needs to file for such in civil court. However, consider the benefit to such a saint, as well as

---

9   See Matthew 5:32.

the local church, of involving the congregation before it ever gets to that stage. If the saint lays out the evidence of adultery before the church, brethren can help him or her determine the will of the Lord. The erring spouse can be rebuked, edified and maybe even restored. In cases where there is only suspicion and not evidence, a great mistake, or even sin, can be avoided. And if divorce is the only or appropriate answer, the sinned against Christian will have the understanding and support of his fellow saints.

Unfortunately, this is not what commonly happens. Often the local church doesn't even know a problem exists until some of the members read in the newspaper of an action filed or decision rendered by civil or criminal courts. If the congregation is engaged in the matter at all, it is often "after the fact," as one or both parties seek approval from the congregation for what has already been done in the heathen courts.

But in the situation that is the subject of this study, namely, a post-legal but completely unscriptural divorce, where the one doing the putting away subsequently commits adultery, it appears to me that the *only* remedy open to a wrongly divorced Christian is the procedure outlined previously, or something similar. I say something similar because not all who find themselves in this predicament will be members of a local church that agrees that a legally divorced innocent party still has the right to put a fornicating mate away. In other situations, a person may not even be a Christian. Nevertheless, the truly innocent party, Christian or otherwise, who has been legally but unscripturally put away by a mate who subsequently commits adultery, and who knows what God has said about MDR, will want to exercise his or her right to put away the fornicating mate. But without the support and judgment of a local church, such an individual would be in a most precarious situation. Even so, there will be those in his immediate community he would want to inform as to what he believes to be his

God-given right to repudiate a fornicating mate and marry again without sin.

But if his local church or immediate community is not interested in adjudicating/considering the matter, thinking such an idea to be mere foolishness, then the innocent party may have no recourse but to know, and be satisfied in his or her own heart and mind, that he or she is right in repudiating the fornicating mate. Some want to portray this as "mental divorce" because it appears to have taken place only in the mind of the person doing the repudiating. But remember this, brothers and sisters in Christ: *God is a witness to these proceedings and the only ratification that really matters (i.e., the only one that is really binding) is God's ratification.* Consequently, when it is thought that it is the ratification of the Church, the State, or the Community *alone* that makes a divorce legitimate in God's sight, God has been usurped and there is a pretender sitting on His throne. This is, as I've tried to point out in this study, nothing but idolatry. The fact that most in our day are dubious of such a claim may tell us more about ourselves than we really want to know.

With this in view, it will do us well to remember that the Lord of the *then*, *now* and *not yet* knows exactly those who are, and *are not*, His[10]—He *always has* and He *always will*. At the same time, those who honor the State as supreme receive "a mark on their right hand and on their foreheads,"[11] which I think means they are wrongly influenced to *do* and *think* those things that are ungodly. In Revelation 13:16-18, this is identified as the mark or name of the beast, or "666," if you will. Is it any wonder, then, that the Lord asked his followers, "Nevertheless, when the Son of Man comes,

---

10 See Revelation 14.
11 Revelation 13:16.

will He really find faith on the earth?"[12] If He could ask this about events surrounding A.D. 70 and the destruction of Jerusalem, might not He ask the same question concerning His final coming? It is certainly worth thinking about, particularly as we consider this subject, for no one has the right to supplant God and His word—absolutely no one, especially the State.

12 Luke 18:8.

Chapter 13

Living In A
Post-Christian World

I believe the Modern Church, in too many instances, has become nothing much more than a sanctified country club of like-minded individuals who have a deeply held desire to be religious and in communion with God while wanting, at the same time, to feel free to exercise themselves as completely autonomous individuals. Such individualism encompasses a multitude of sins. Nevertheless, I think this kind of thinking directly impinges the subject of MDR, speaking to why the church sometimes doesn't even know there's a problem in a marriage until someone has already filed for a divorce in civil court. In yet other cases, such is not revealed until after a divorce is final.

So let's just think about all this for a moment. What does this kind of person think the church of Christ stands for? Does he think it's just some accouterment that exists to validate his individual autonomy and freedoms while all the while making him feel good about himself? If this were the case, then such a church would no longer have the right to call itself "of Christ." Actually, "of Belial" would be a much more appropriate description. In other words, true New Testament Christianity can be true to itself only if it is willing to be iconoclastic. By this I mean that if the church belonging to Christ has any hope of doing what it has been called by the Lord to do, it must be willing to be actively engaged in breaking to pieces the world's idols, and this would, for certain, include demystifying the State by rejecting any form of Babelism/Statism

In other words, one clear function of the church belonging to Christ in any age is to unmask the idols and expose them for what they really are—i.e., nothing but sham gods. There is no other basis for doing so than the truths contained in God's Word. With this in mind, notice that the apostle Paul, in 1 Timothy 3:15, exclaimed the "House of God, which is the church of the living God," is nothing less than "the pillar and ground of the truth." This means, among other things, that the pathologies that were present in the pre-Christian world[1] (viz., the economic, social, familial, sexual, and legal aspects of life) are very much alive in our post-Christian world.[2] Consequently, the truths taught in the Bible, particularly those found in the New Testament, are especially meaningful to our post-Christian culture, not just because they are God's truths, but because they were written in the midst of a pre-Christian society. Thus, we are today in a position to read the truths of the Bible within basically the same context in which they were written.[3]

Consequently, American Christians, like African and Asian Christians in the last few generations, are duty bound to see themselves as subversives in an alien culture. That this has proved to be most difficult for Christians living in America is an understatement. Why? Because our society, although a cut-flower generation, is still sustained by the Christian and Biblical nutrients that were originally derived from its founding roots. It is, therefore,

---

[1] By "pre-Christian world," I mean a world that is predominantly pagan in its outlook.

[2] Again, by "post-Christian world" I mean, as was explained previously, a society that has been almost totally secularized, as ours was during the last third of the previous century.

[3] Although our present culture is not pagan *per se*, it is nevertheless neo-pagan in its outlook.

most unpalatable for an American who is a Christian to think of his or her country as the alien neo-pagan nation it really is. Even so, the invitation addressed to those who made up the pre-Christian culture of the first century was, "Be saved from this perverse generation."[4] Living, as we are, in a post-Christian world, we are called upon to do the very same thing.

Thus, it behooves us to pay closer attention to the book of John and related portions of the New Testament. There "the world" is described as the system of political, cultural, and religious leadership that stood against God and refused to listen to the preaching and teaching that exposed its injustices and unrighteousness. It is this kind of world that Jesus said "hates Me because I testify of it that its works are evil."[5] The writers of the New Testament realized that the followers of Jesus Christ were no different in this respect from their Lord: "Do you not know that friendship with the world is enmity with God? Whoever therefore wants to be a friend of the world makes himself an enemy of God."[6] Thus, Paul's description of a sinful lifestyle was living "according to the course of this world, according to the prince of the power of the air, the spirit who now works in the sons of disobedience."[7]

Of course, even when the lines are not drawn so clearly between the gospel of Christ and an adulterous environment, as they now are in our post-Christian society, an inevitable strain will always exist between Biblical faith and culture.[8] As long as the Biblical world view is not identical with any other religious, cultural, or

---

4   Acts 2:40.
5   John 7:7.
6   James 4:4.
7   Ephesians 2:2.
8   By saying this I don't mean to imply that I think these lines are clear in the minds of those deluded by secularism. They are not. Nevertheless, those not unduly influenced by secularism should be able to see this quite easily.

political systems (and this will always be the case), any effort to relax the tension between them, accommodating pure New Testament Christianity to the "best" of the surrounding society, surrenders the gospel to the very thing that debases it. Therefore, the preachers of "Peace, peace! When there is no peace,"[9] spout theologies of harmony designed to avoid conflict at any cost. This produces a dumbed-down church that is tamed and ineffective, and one that doesn't have a clue regarding its own idolatries.[10] If one stretches this template over the American Church, then he is able to see more clearly, at least in part, the problem that plagues us today.

Churches of Christ in America are being absorbed by their culture. Instead of being the penetrating leaven that leavens the culture around us, as Matthew 13:33 says we should, we are being eaten alive by the world's influences. Instead of walking circumspectly, as Ephesians 5:15 requires, we are first blinded, then mesmerized, by the "isms" of our day, much like the deer caught in the headlights. Many Christians living at the beginning of the twenty-first century, instead of being the totally unique people that 1 Peter 2:9 calls upon us to be, are a denuded bunch of spiritual and intellectual miscreants. It is time for most churches (as individual Christians and collectively) to regroup, strictly patterning themselves according to the truths contained in God's word, so they can be the iconoclasts the Lord Jesus called them to be. This will not be an easy task. But if we are determined to make the effort, then God will enable us to do exactly what He created us in Christ Jesus to do.

---

9 Jeremiah 6:14.
10 I'm speaking of the seeker-friendly, market oriented "church as you want it" that has become so prevalent in our culture.

Patriotism: Idolatry or Effective Service?

The subject of "patriotism" offers another example of what I'm talking about. Christians in the pre-Christian world were, for the most part, citizens of the nation in which they resided. They were required by the Lord to be not just good citizens, but exemplary ones as well. Even so, the Bible does not teach that one's citizenship obligations should ever interfere with the Christian's duty to obey God rather than men.[11] Thus, there are times when a Christian must refuse to serve his country, and if he didn't, he would certainly be involving himself in sin. In other words, and as I've tried to point out frequently in this study, the State does not possess ultimate authority. Whatever authority it possesses is the delegated kind,[12] and any government that doesn't recognize this is idolatrous. Consequently, whatever patriotism is, it cannot—indeed, it must not—automatically exempt itself from the charge that "in his own eyes he flatters himself too much to detect or hate his sin."[13] Whatever it is, patriotism should not suppose that by invoking the name of God in slogans it will tether the Most High God to its cause any more successfully than rebellious Israel did when Eli's sons took the ark of the covenant out of mothballs and propped it like a talisman before the armies marching against the Philistines.[14]

True patriotism does not permit itself to be manipulated by media mantras into a pumped-up frenzy that drowns out all other voices, particularly the voice of Jesus, who said, "Render to Caesar what is Caesar's and to God what is God's." To the State, then, obedient servants present their bodies and wills for the national

---

11 See Acts 5:29.
12 See John 19:11.
13 Psalm 36:2, NIV.
14 See 1 Samuel 4.

defense only so long as such a defense is consistent with the truths taught in God's Word; to God, of course, they must always present a "contrite and humble spirit."[15] As a result, there need be no contradiction, no conflict of interest, between Church and State unless, and until, the State commands the Christian to do something God has prohibited, or else forbids something God has commanded. So, like Daniel, who knew how to "seek the peace of the city" to which God had carried him into exile,[16] but who, along with Hananiah, Mishael and Azariah, would not bow to its "image of gold,"[17] the New Testament Christian needs to reflect the godly patriotism the Lord enjoins for His priesthood of spiritual pilgrims who, in every age, sojourn in Babylon while "longing for a better country."[18] "Pray," He says in Jeremiah 29:7b, "to the Lord for [your country]; for in its peace you will have peace."

Therefore, I do not believe the only choice of action for the thinking Christian is found in the tweedledee of mindless, hysterical hawkishness, or the tweedledum of half-baked, limpish pacifism. Instead, there ought to be a loyalty to one's country based on truth, not lies, and a manly, unflinching patriotism that is based on reality and not popular fiction. The causes of Justice and Righteousness today, like always, call for civil servants (especially soldiers and policemen) who are prudent, courageous, self-controlled and just. These need to possess the virtues that will enable them to know not just why and when to go to war, but how to properly fight it, and finally, when to stop it. We need soldiers, particularly, who are distinguished by the kind of character that empowers them to pursue every honorable avenue for victory against the

---

15 Isaiah 57:15.
16 See Jeremiah 29:7a.
17 Daniel 3.
18 Hebrews 11:16, NIV.

enemy, but who are, in the end, resolved to suffer death before dishonor. Where better to find this character and these virtues than in the Christian? The Christian fights for Justice because God is like this, in that He uses force to check evil and bring Justice. So, the Christian uses force to restrain evil because this is what God is like, and because God is like this, the Christian does not sin when he uses legitimate force, and this remains true even when this force is deadly force.

What's more, as God's use of force is a product of His love for His creatures, and as it is clear that God even loves those whom He kills, the Christian, just like God, must love his enemies even when called upon to kill them. Any acts that do not appear to be God-like will be morally suspect for the Christian soldier. This means the acts of a soldier can never be ones of personal vengeance, as Matthew 5:38-41 point out. Therefore, a just war is something Christians participate in out of loving obedience to God and in conformity to His ways. In his personal relationships, the Christian acts in love toward others as God has always required His followers to do. But when he chooses to participate in government as a soldier or law enforcement officer, he acts in accord with the God-ordained mandate given to the State.

There is no contradiction here, as the Christian is free to participate in any legitimate function of government, even war, without violating the restrictions God places on him in his personal affairs. On the other hand, those who think the Christian, simply by virtue of his Christianity, gets to opt out of doing Justice are sorely mistaken. They fail, in their elitism, to comprehend what being a faithful subject of God is all about.[19] As such, they delegate the "dirty hands" duty of doing Justice to unredeemed sinners. In

---

19 See Micah 8:8 and Matthew 23:23.

doing so, they fail to fully understand the nature of God (a nature that demands Justice) and denigrate the very character of those people God has appointed over the administration of Justice—people the apostle Paul called "ministers to you for good."

Living the Christian life is difficult and complex. The vagaries are many. Decisions involving the *when, where* and *how* of the Christian's participation *with* or *in* society and government are difficult. As we've seen from this study, brethren don't always draw the line between Church and State in the same place, and all attempts to do so are arduous in nature. The "yoke is easy" and the "burden is light" only when compared to the glorious reward that awaits us in heaven.[20] The line between Church and State cannot be correctly drawn apart from rightly dividing God's word. It is, therefore, unfortunate that many of God's people, past and present, because they have failed to rightly divide God's word, as 2 Timothy 2:15 requires, have majored in the theology of calling good evil and evil good.[21] Can a Christian participate in war? Yes, when the doing of Justice demands it. Can a Christian participate in just any war? No, he cannot. If the war is not morally justified, and by this I mean consistent with the precepts and principles taught in the Bible, a Christian would not remain "unspotted" by participating in it. What's more, a Christian could not participate even in a just war if the means being used to fight it are not just. Consequently, the Christian must always sit in judgment upon the activities of his government, supporting it when it is right, but refusing to do so when it is wrong. This, I believe, is part of what being a true Christian is all about. Anyone interested in plumbing the depths of this issue more thoroughly should see *The Christian*

---

[20] See Matthew 11:29-30; 16:24-27.
[21] See Isaiah 5:20.

& War, a book I wrote and published in 2006, along with the rather extensive study provided at www.allanturner.com/War.pdf.

The Christian's Obligation Is Never Easy

A Christian's obligation to the State, whether it be in the case of patriotism or MDR, is all too frequently an agonizingly difficult task. The more a government reflects the Revelation 13 model (rather than the Romans 13 one), the more agonizing such choices will be. A government could become so evil that a Christian could no longer assist it—as a soldier or anything else—and maintain his integrity. Just where to draw the line will, except in the most extreme of cases, be difficult for the civically conscious Christian. After all is said and done, it will be the individual Christian's conscience, hopefully properly schooled by the truths taught in God's Word, that must guide him in what he can and cannot do concerning his duties and obligations to government and society. Nevertheless, we cannot forget that somewhere in this process the Christian could become identified with the "mark of the beast." Prayerfully, and circumspectly, the Christian will seek to safely navigate the treacherous shoals of Church-State issues regardless of the particular subject at hand.

Thus, I find it interesting, perhaps even ironic, that most brethren who disagree with me on whether or not a Christian can be a law enforcement officer or soldier have not sought to withdraw their fellowship from me, even though they strongly disagree with my position; but have, on the other hand, resorted to calling my position on MDR "heresy," and this in spite of the fact that we are much more in agreement on MDR than we are on whether it is permissible for a Christian to be a policeman or soldier. As a matter of fact, I don't know of anything my opponents and I disagree on concerning MDR than the fact that a legal divorce for just any cause (viz., no-fault divorce), although possible in this day and age (as it was in the first century), does not really count in dissolving the bonds of matrimony. This makes us, I think, just about ninety-nine and nine tenths percent in agreement. Of course, I realize this one tenth is not unimportant, and I have presented my case as to why I think it is not unimportant.

What's more, I have not ignored what I clearly see to be issues that could arise in a local church causing a break in fellowship on this subject; but I have honestly worked hard, at least I have thought so, at not trying to divide folks on this issue while it is being studied. I have always known that a break in fellowship was possible either because I would not be able to be a part of a local church that refused to recognize a Christian's right to put away a fornicating mate after a legal (but unscriptural) divorce had been granted at the behest of the now fornicating mate, or because my position on MDR could cause a local church to withdraw its fellowship from me. Even so, I have not failed to preach and teach what I believe to be the truth on this subject. Although Christians have disagreed with me, and I with them, I have never been prohibited from preaching what I believed the Bible teaches on this. However, it appears to me that a charge of heresy does not bode well for continued fellowship. It seems clear that some are now ready to divide over this issue. In some places this has already occurred and we may see much more of this as some seem bound and determined to defend what they consider to be orthodoxy and what I consider to be a doctrine included in the "doctrines of demons" mentioned in 1 Timothy 4:1-3. But here's the question I want you to consider: When it comes to orthodoxy, whose orthodoxy are we talking about? Yes, what the Bible teaches on this subject must be obeyed and defended, and I certainly believe there is a correct (i.e., an orthodox) position on MDR, and to the best of my ability I'm trying to teach it. Others (in this case, perhaps the majority of my brethren) disagree with me. Who is right? The answer to this question is what this study is all about, for how can we know what is right unless we are willing to thoroughly, patiently, carefully, and honestly study this issue out?

Conservative, non-institutional brethren did not like it one bit when liberal, institutional brethren vilified them as "Antis," believing, as I do as well, that such an epithet did not accurately identify the position being defended and served to unduly prejudice those on the other side against it. Today, the "Anti" moniker continues to do just that. It flows off the tongues of many of our institutional brethren like a dirty word. "You're not an 'Anti,' are you?," they say with horrified looks on their faces. This is not far removed from similar expressions one sees on the faces of those who exclaim, "You're not a 'mental divorcer,' are you?" Just as many of our liberal brethren don't have a clue as to what we so-called "Antis" believe and practice on this subject, many who use the term "mental divorcer" don't have a clue as to what I believe and practice, or why. So, now you know.

In Conclusion

I would like to think that all who have read this defense are now in agreement with me. But reality-based thinking causes me to believe that many of you will still disagree with my conclusions. Therefore, in closing, I want to make it clear to you that I remain ready and open to discussing this subject, either privately or publicly, all the while hoping and praying that such discussions will be informative, constructive, and honorable. Feel free to accurately identify and Biblically critique my position, but I ask you to please refrain from the vilification, name calling and innuendo so common in the carnal arsenal of the heathens. For those who need a refresher course on what I'm referring to, take a look at 2 Corinthians 10:14.

Criticism that appeals to God's Word does not offend me. Please remember that I am not a straw man.[22] Therefore, I plead with those who disagree with me to address my arguments and not those reflecting the various constructs some have devised to refute what they call the "mental divorce" position. If you will do this, you will have earned my respect, whether I agree with you or not, and perhaps you will be successful in convincing me that I am wrong. But if you continue to believe I am a heretic or apostate, don't just say so, be willing to prove it with Scripture.

On the other hand, if you are an idolater of the sort I have mentioned in this study, don't get mad at me because I have brought this to your attention. Instead, think about repenting while you still have time and opportunity.

Finally, my fervent prayer is that a gracious God will continue to bless us all in our study of His Word and that He will, in the days to come, be able to bless America, as He has surely done in the past.

---

[22] The Straw Man fallacy is committed when one simply ignores a person's actual position and substitutes a distorted, exaggerated or misrepresented version of it.

Appendix

In Congress, July 4, 1776

The unanimous Declaration of the thirteen united States of America[1]

When in the Course of human events it becomes necessary for one people to dissolve the political bands which have connected them with another and to assume among the powers of the earth, the separate and equal station to which the Laws of Nature and of Nature's God entitle them, a decent respect to the opinions of mankind requires that they should declare the causes which impel them to the separation.

We hold these truths to be self-evident, that all men are created equal, that they are endowed by their Creator with certain unalienable Rights, that among these are Life, Liberty and the pursuit of Happiness. — That to secure these rights, Governments are instituted among Men, deriving their just powers from the consent of the governed, — That whenever any Form of Government becomes destructive of these ends, it is the Right of the People to alter or to abolish it, and to institute new Government, laying its foundation on such principles and organizing its powers in such form, as to them shall seem most likely to effect their Safety and

---

[1] This is the complete text of the *Declaration of Independence*. The original spelling, capitalization, and punctuation have been retained.

Happiness. Prudence, indeed, will dictate that Governments long established should not be changed for light and transient causes; and accordingly all experience hath shewn that mankind are more disposed to suffer, while evils are sufferable than to right themselves by abolishing the forms to which they are accustomed. But when a long train of abuses and usurpations, pursuing invariably the same Object evinces a design to reduce them under absolute Despotism, it is their right, it is their duty, to throw off such Government, and to provide new Guards for their future security. — Such has been the patient sufferance of these Colonies; and such is now the necessity which constrains them to alter their former Systems of Government. The history of the present King of Great Britain is a history of repeated injuries and usurpations, all having in direct object the establishment of an absolute Tyranny over these States. To prove this, let Facts be submitted to a candid world.

He has refused his Assent to Laws, the most wholesome and necessary for the public good.

He has forbidden his Governors to pass Laws of immediate and pressing importance, unless suspended in their operation till his Assent should be obtained; and when so suspended, he has utterly neglected to attend to them.

He has refused to pass other Laws for the accommodation of large districts of people, unless those people would relinquish the right of Representation in the Legislature, a right inestimable to them and formidable to tyrants only.

He has called together legislative bodies at places unusual, uncomfortable, and distant from the depository of their Public Records, for the sole purpose of fatiguing them into compliance with his measures.

He has dissolved Representative Houses repeatedly, for opposing with manly firmness his invasions on the rights of the people.

He has refused for a long time, after such dissolutions, to cause others to be elected, whereby the Legislative Powers, incapable of Annihilation, have returned to the People at large for their exercise; the state remaining in the mean time exposed to all the dangers of invasion from without, and convulsions within.

He has endeavoured to prevent the population of these States; for that purpose obstructing the Laws for Naturalization of Foreigners; refusing to pass others to encourage their migrations hither, and raising the conditions of new Appropriations of Lands.

He has obstructed the Administration of Justice by refusing his Assent to Laws for establishing Judiciary Powers.

He has made Judges dependent on his Will alone for the tenure of their offices, and the amount and payment of their salaries.

He has erected a multitude of New Offices, and sent hither swarms of Officers to harass our people and eat out their substance.

He has kept among us, in times of peace, Standing Armies without the Consent of our legislatures.

He has affected to render the Military independent of and superior to the Civil Power.

He has combined with others to subject us to a jurisdiction foreign to our constitution, and unacknowledged by our laws; giving his Assent to their Acts of pretended Legislation:

For quartering large bodies of armed troops among us:

For protecting them, by a mock Trial from punishment for any Murders which they should commit on the Inhabitants of these States:

For cutting off our Trade with all parts of the world:

For imposing Taxes on us without our Consent:

For depriving us in many cases, of the benefit of Trial by Jury:

For transporting us beyond Seas to be tried for pretended offences:

For abolishing the free System of English Laws in a neighbouring Province, establishing therein an Arbitrary government, and enlarging its Boundaries so as to render it at once an example and fit instrument for introducing the same absolute rule into these Colonies:

For taking away our Charters, abolishing our most valuable Laws and altering fundamentally the Forms of our Governments:

For suspending our own Legislatures, and declaring themselves invested with power to legislate for us in all cases whatsoever.

He has abdicated Government here, by declaring us out of his Protection and waging War against us.

He has plundered our seas, ravaged our coasts, burnt our towns, and destroyed the lives of our people.

He is at this time transporting large Armies of foreign Mercenaries to compleat the works of death, desolation, and tyranny, already begun with circumstances of Cruelty & Perfidy scarcely paralleled in the most barbarous ages, and totally unworthy the Head of a civilized nation.

He has constrained our fellow Citizens taken Captive on the high Seas to bear Arms against their Country, to become the executioners of their friends and Brethren, or to fall themselves by their Hands.

He has excited domestic insurrections amongst us, and has endeavoured to bring on the inhabitants of our frontiers, the merciless Indian Savages whose known rule of warfare, is an undistinguished destruction of all ages, sexes and conditions.

In every stage of these Oppressions We have Petitioned for Redress in the most humble terms: Our repeated Petitions have been answered only by repeated injury. A Prince, whose character is thus marked by every act which may define a Tyrant, is unfit to be the ruler of a free people.

Nor have We been wanting in attentions to our British brethren. We have warned them from time to time of attempts by their legislature to extend an unwarrantable jurisdiction over us. We have reminded them of the circumstances of our emigration and settlement here. We have appealed to their native justice and magnanimity, and we have conjured them by the ties of our common kindred to disavow these usurpations, which would inevitably interrupt our connections and correspondence. They too have been deaf to the voice of justice and of consanguinity. We must, therefore, acquiesce in the necessity, which denounces our Separation, and hold them, as we hold the rest of mankind, Enemies in War, in Peace Friends.

We, therefore, the Representatives of the united States of America, in General Congress, Assembled, appealing to the Supreme Judge of the world for the rectitude of our intentions, do, in the Name, and by Authority of the good People of these Colonies, solemnly publish and declare, That these united Colonies are, and of Right ought to be Free and Independent States, that they are Absolved from all Allegiance to the British Crown, and that all political connection between them and the State of Great Britain, is and ought to be totally dissolved; and that as Free and Independent States, they have full Power to levy War, conclude Peace, contract Alliances, establish Commerce, and to do all other Acts and Things which Independent States may of right do. — And for the support of this Declaration, with a firm reliance on the protection of Divine Providence, we mutually pledge to each other our Lives, our Fortunes, and our sacred Honor.

— John Hancock

New Hampshire:
Josiah Bartlett, William Whipple, Matthew Thornton

Massachusetts:
John Hancock, Samuel Adams, John Adams, Robert Treat
Paine, Elbridge Gerry

Rhode Island:
Stephen Hopkins, William Ellery

Connecticut:
Roger Sherman, Samuel Huntington, William Williams, Oliver Wolcott

New York:
William Floyd, Philip Livingston, Francis Lewis, Lewis
Morris

New Jersey:
Richard Stockton, John Witherspoon, Francis Hopkinson,
John Hart, Abraham Clark

Pennsylvania:
Robert Morris, Benjamin Rush, Benjamin Franklin, John
Morton, George Clymer, James Smith, George Taylor, James Wilson, George Ross

Delaware:
Caesar Rodney, George Read, Thomas McKean

Maryland:

Samuel Chase, William Paca, Thomas Stone, Charles Carroll of Carrollton

Virginia:
George Wythe, Richard Henry Lee, Thomas Jefferson, Benjamin Harrison, Thomas Nelson, Jr., Francis Lightfoot Lee, Carter Braxton

North Carolina:
William Hooper, Joseph Hewes, John Penn

South Carolina:
Edward Rutledge, Thomas Heyward, Jr., Thomas Lynch, Jr., Arthur Middleton

Georgia:
Button Gwinnett, Lyman Hall, George Walton

Index

Other Books By Allan Turner

The Christian & War (ISBN: 0-9777350-0-1)
The Christian & War E-book (ISBN: 0-9777350-1-X)
The Christian & Idolatry (ISBN: 0-9777350-2-8)
The Christian & Calvinism (ISBN:0-9777350-3-6)

Allan Turner's Personal Web Site

www.allanturner.com

ALLANITA PRESS PUBLISHING

www.allanitapress.com

ALLANITA PRESS
PUBLISHING